T0299443

CATALOGUE OF
THE MUSICAL MANUSCRIPTS
AT PETERHOUSE
CAMBRIDGE

CATALOGUE
OF THE
MUSICAL MANUSCRIPTS
AT PETERHOUSE
CAMBRIDGE

COMPILED BY

DOM ANSELM HUGHES
M.A., F.S.A.
Monk of Nashdom

CAMBRIDGE
AT THE UNIVERSITY PRESS
1953

CAMBRIDGE
UNIVERSITY PRESS

University Printing House, Cambridge CB2 8BS, United Kingdom

Cambridge University Press is part of the University of Cambridge.

It furthers the University's mission by disseminating knowledge in the pursuit of education, learning and research at the highest international levels of excellence.

www.cambridge.org
Information on this title: www.cambridge.org/9781107544666

© Cambridge University Press 1953

First published 1953
First paperback edition 2015

A catalogue record for this publication is available from the British Library

ISBN 978-1-107-54466-6 Paperback

CONTENTS

INTRODUCTION

Materials for the history of Church music in England before 1662 are not so plentiful as we might desire. Among the more obvious reasons for their relative scarcity are the two upheavals of religious practice, first in the middle of the sixteenth century, and again in Commonwealth days, both accompanied by senseless and sacrilegious raids in which quantities of musical manuscripts were lost and destroyed.

There is a third reason which is perhaps not so widely realized, and it is hardly too much to say that the careful preservation of antiquities is a comparatively modern turn of thought and habit. There are, of course, numerous exceptions to this generalization, but these are due to illustrious individuals—a Camden, a Hearne; and the common temper of past centuries was to throw out manuscript music as waste so soon as anything more modern was ready for use. For this reason the earlier musical history of England is largely built up upon such things as the thirteenth- and fourteenth-century Worcester music,[1] used as guard-leaves by the Chapter's binders in the fifteenth century, or the music written in the reign of Henry V and turned into wrappers for documents at Fountains Abbey as early as 1446,[2] or that of slightly later date used for a like purpose in the archiepiscopal probate registry at York. Among the documentary sources which remain from the period running from about 1540 to 1640 the Peterhouse manuscripts stand out prominently as having escaped these destructive events and tendencies.

Nineteen in number, they fall into two well-defined groups: (i) a set of four Latin part-books, described hereafter as 'The Henrician set'; and (ii) two sets of English part-books with some Latin insertions, which we refer to as 'The Caroline sets'; together with a contemporary Organ-Book. Fifteen of these

---

[1] Hughes, *Worcester Mediaeval Harmony* (1928).
[2] British Museum, MS. Addit. 40011 B.

nineteen were catalogued fully in 1856 by John Jebb, then rector of Peterstow in Herefordshire. His manuscript catalogue is in the Perne Library, and it has been extensively used in making this work ready for press. As the Henrician and Caroline sets are period pieces of the sixteenth and seventeenth centuries, so is Jebb's list for the nineteenth, written as it is with loving care (though, as we shall notice occasionally, not with complete accuracy) in a style which is mannered without being pompous. Three years later (1859) Jebb printed his list, without the folio numbers, in *The Ecclesiologist*.[1] The existence of this printed catalogue was perhaps the reason why Dr M. R. James omitted the musical manuscripts from his *Catalogue of the Manuscripts at Peterhouse* (1899). The 1859 catalogue is itself scarce, nor did Jebb give a list of the items in the Organ-Book; moreover, as narrated below, three more part-books of one of the Caroline sets have been unearthed in recent years, making it even more desirable for an up-to-date catalogue to be prepared. Numerous corrections and additions to the older list have been necessary, but without the industrious toil of Dr Jebb the present compiler could neither have undertaken nor carried out the preparation of this edition.

THE HENRICIAN SET

The Henrician part-books consist of four out of a set of five, Triplex, Medius, Contratenor, and Bassus: the Tenor book is missing. They were rebound at some time between 1856 and 1883[2] and numbered 40, 41, 31, 32 respectively. When the rebinding of these and eleven of the Caroline books was done, the volumes were apparently numbered quite arbitrarily without reference to the sequence of their contents. From the inclusion of music by Christopher Tye (*c.* 1497–1572/3), Thomas Tallis (*c.* 1505–85), and John Marbeck (*c.* 1510–85), and from the absence of any compositions by William Byrd (1543–1623),

[1] Vol. xx, pp. 163, 242: 'Mr. Jebb's Catalogue of Ancient Choirbooks at S. Peter's College, Cambridge.'

[2] R. C. Hope, in 'An unique MS. collection of Ancient Church Music' (*Antiquarian Magazine and Bibliographer*, vol. iii, 1883, p. 24), says that the rebinding was done before that time and subsequent to the preparation of Jebb's catalogue. Hope's article is no more than a précis of Jebb's work and contains no fresh information except for this point about the rebinding.

Causton, or Shepherd, and from the lack of any other post-Reformation in-
dications, their date can be assigned with reasonable certainty to the later part
of the reign of Henry VIII. Were it not for the style of the notation ('black full')
the reign of Queen Mary might be equally possible, but the 'black full' notation
had given way everywhere to 'black void' by the middle of the century. They
can hardly be much earlier than 1540, on account of the composers included:
and by 1542 or 1543 the shadows of impending changes would have made it
quite unlikely for further undertakings of this kind to be begun on so considerable a scale. The part-books are all in excellent condition and give the impression
(in sharp contrast to the Caroline sets) of being fresh unused copies. Their date,
if taken at about 1540, is entirely consonant with the idea of a set of choir-books
being written so soon before the proscription of the Latin services that they
were never put into use. A comparison of the mass *O quam glorifica* by Robert
Fayrfax with the earlier copy at Lambeth[1] reveals a number of small mistakes in
the Peterhouse books which would surely have been corrected had they actually
been used in choir.

The extent of our losses caused by the disappearance of the tenor book can
be summarized as follows:

The tenor parts of the music of Aston, Taverner, and Tallis are available from
other sources and have been so provided by the editors of *Tudor Church Music*,
with full information as to those sources. With the exception of the motets *Lauda
vivi* and *O Maria Deo grata*, which still lack their tenors, the works by Fayrfax
are found partially or entire in manuscripts at Caius College, Chelmsford,
Lambeth, Oxford, and Tenbury.[2] All five parts of Rasar's mass are in the
Bodleian Library at Oxford.[3] Ludford's mass *Christi virgo* is in Caius College
MS. 667, but the other two masses by him and his four motets, together with
all the rest of the Peterhouse collection, still remain incomplete.

From its earliest existence in the thirteenth century up to 1634, when Matthew
Wren built the College chapel, Peterhouse used the adjoining parish church of
Little St Mary for its services. A corridor leading from the college to the
church still exists, and it is used on special occasions such as the institution of
a new vicar, the Master and Fellows being patrons of the benefice. About the

[1] Lambeth Palace, Archiepiscopal Library, MS. 1.
[2] For details see *Music and Letters* (April 1949), p. 118.
[3] MSS. Mus. Sch. e 376–80.

college music of this period nothing is known. The four Latin part-books suggest at first sight a collegiate choir with a high degree of skill and proficiency; but of this there is no record. On the other hand at the time the first Buttery Book was begun (29 September 1542) the numbers had sunk as low as 25 (the Master, nine Fellows, one ex-Fellow, five probationary Fellows and nine undergraduates). A similar state of depression is found at that time throughout the colleges of Oxford as well as of Cambridge. Though it is possible that these Latin books belonged to and were designed for a Peterhouse choir, or for Little St Mary's, before 1547 it seems on the whole unlikely. They may have been procured during the reign of Queen Mary, or they may have been acquired during the period of considerable musical activity in the early seventeenth century.

THE CAROLINE SETS

The Caroline part-books are fourteen in number. They belong to two distinct sets, originally containing ten and eight volumes respectively. For want of better terms, they are distinguished throughout this catalogue as the Former and the Latter sets, though there is really little difference in their dates, if any. But the distinction has been made on these lines because the Latter set contains a good deal of music composed by Molle and Wilson, the former of whom was probably, and the latter certainly, organist of Peterhouse; and it is therefore more like a current collection of the Cosin era between 1635 and 1643, the only period in which we know this music to have been used; whereas the Former set may perhaps have been assembled a little earlier. Thomas Wilson is styled 'Organista Petrensis' in the Bass Cantoris book of the Latter set; as to his date all that can be said is that his 'Venite' is dated 1636, and that he is quite likely to be the Mr Wilson to whom 13s. 4d. was repaid in the Chapel accounts on 25 October 1642 for 'Res musica'. An organist's post was established on 12 November 1635 by a 'Decretum de Organista et ejus stipendiis', with the duty of instructing and training the 'pauperes scholares' in sacred music, and playing in chapel on feast-days and their first evensongs. References to the stipend of the organists occur in the accounts from 1637 to 1642/3, when the stipend ceases: in the Buttery Book the attendance of the organist is recorded, sometimes regularly, sometimes spasmodically, from about June 1636 until 17 November 1643. Wilson is also described as organist of Peterhouse by the editors of *Tudor Church Music*:[1] but their statement which follows—'The books [*sc.* the Caroline sets] were completed in the time of Henry Loosemore after the Restoration'—rests on no particular evidence and is not in general accord with the contents. No purely post-Restoration composer is included (the identification of Cranford is quite uncertain): Child and Loosemore are the only two of our Caroline composers who are known to have continued their musical careers after the Restoration, and of these Loosemore had been organist of King's for seven years before Cosin's arrival at Peterhouse in 1634, while Child was appointed to Windsor in 1630 as a lay-clerk and in 1632 as organist and master of the choristers.

The Caroline sets are quite unlike the Henrician books in that they are collections of separate bifolia or other small gatherings, with some single fly-leaves, in many cases bearing the original page or folio numbers (usually cancelled) of earlier collections to which they once belonged. There is no possible doubt that they are the actual books used in the chapel of Peterhouse up to about 1643. Their well-worn condition, untidy at first sight, reveals on close examination a sort of rough laborious efficiency and accuracy. They are working tools which show abundant signs of toil and long service, and a great part of their contents must have been in use well before 1635. Taverner's 'Sine nomine' mass, for example, is in a mid-sixteenth-century hand. There seems to be no evidence from College records or elsewhere to show whether the earlier matter included in these volumes would have been used in Little St Mary's before the Peterhouse chapel was built. Much of the music may have been acquired in second-hand condition in 1635 or thereabouts, and in the Chapel accounts there appears a sum of £40 expended soon after upon 'Libri Chorales',[2] which may include either of these sets: it is rather too large a sum in the values of that period to be responsible for nothing more than eight or ten part-books.

The numerous pieces of music by local organists, some of them autograph, such as Amner (Ely, 1610–41), Loosemore (King's, 1627–44, and from the Restoration until 1670), and Ramsey (Trinity, 1628–44) lend colour to the idea that the books were assembled from miscellaneous acquisitions after the building of the chapel and the appointment of an organist; so also does the music by

---

[1] Vol. II, p. xxiii. [2] T. A. Walker, *Peterhouse* (1935), p. 128.

Hutchinson and the two Smiths, which was very likely brought from Durham to Cambridge by Cosin, or procured thence by him: he had been a prebendary of Durham for ten years before his election as Master of Peterhouse in 1634. Several of these hands are distinguishable, that of Amner, an excellent piece of calligraphy, being the most obvious. Loosemore's writings appear to be signed by him, but in other cases of a name appended to a composition it may occasionally happen that the scribe is merely continuing the fifteenth- and sixteenth-century custom of entering the composer's name at the end.

The composition of these two sets will best be explained in tabular form:

THE FORMER SET			THE LATTER SET	
DECANI	MS.		DECANI	MS.
Medius	(not numbered)		Medius	44
Contratenor I	39		Contratenor	42
Contratenor II	(not numbered)			
Tenor	(lost)		Tenor	43
Bass	38		Bass	37
CANTORIS			CANTORIS	
Medius	34		Medius	45
Contratenor I	(not numbered)		Contratenor	(lost)
Contratenor II	(lost)[1]			
Tenor	(lost)		Tenor	35
Bass	33		Bass	36

The highest voice in all this music bears the name of Medius, which corresponds to the male alto of today, though his range was higher than it is now. The question of a boys' choir in the college chapel does not therefore arise; there is no trace of it in the college records, and all the Peterhouse music of this period is for men's voices only.

[1] Its existence is implied by the arrangement of Adrian Batten's 'Holy, holy, holy' (see p. 12 below).

VOLUMES RECOVERED SINCE 1926

The books for Medius Decani, Contratenor II Decani, and Contratenor I Cantoris of the Former set are not numbered. These are the three manuscripts recovered in the present century, and the story of their finding is suggestive and full of interest.

About 1926 it was discovered by George Witt, a college servant, that behind a panel in the Perne Library was a waste space which had been used either as a cupboard or as a hiding-place at some time in the distant past, so thick with dust and cobwebs that the articles found inside were practically buried. They must have lain undisturbed for a great length of time, for the three unnumbered part-books were so completely hidden that they were not discovered at first, and were in fact found by the former Perne Librarian, Prof. Butterfield, in stages and on successive occasions. They appear to be in their original bindings, bearing an impressed stamp similar to that of the 1638 New Testament in the Perne Library and of the 1639 Prayer Books mentioned below (p. 51). In Jebb's time the eleven volumes of these two Caroline sets which he used in compiling his list were in bindings, in his words, 'of the age of Charles I, black leather with the College Arms and with the designation of the several parts stamped on the side'. This description tallies exactly with the present appearance of the three recovered volumes, and it is difficult to avoid the conclusion that these three have lain concealed from 1642 to 1926. For from about 1642 the Perne Library was certainly used as a hiding-place for furnishings of the Chapel threatened by the oncoming tide of Puritan opposition. The organ pipes were 'laid up and secured' in the College Library, and the 'great Bellowes' were put in the long gallery over the Library. Walker[1] says that the Master and Fellows in the Puritan period

thriftily disposed of the organ pipes and case to a London citizen for £31; and when various articles of Chapel furniture were discovered hidden in the Library, they speedily secularized them. Dr. Francius only saved the Altar hangings by becoming their purchaser. They divided Cosin's service-books among themselves, and dispersed them with such zeal that it was only recently that a single survivor found its way back by purchase to the College.

[1] *Op. cit.* pp. 60–1.

It would seem therefore that the three volumes which were recovered in 1926 were more effectively concealed than those which Jebb knew in 1856, and that while his eleven part-books, with the Henrician set and the Organ-Book, were brought to light at some period between 1661 and 1856, the hiding-place behind the panel had been forgotten until it was found in 1926. Is it too much to hope that yet another place of concealment may be unearthed some day, disclosing some or all of the part-books still missing? The tenor book of the Henrician set in particular would be a most valuable find on account of the many items still incomplete. The Former set, even with the addition of the three newly found volumes, still lacks the tenor book for each side of the choir, besides the Contratenor II Cantoris. In this condition the set is of sadly diminished value, for works not to be found elsewhere are not yet entire. But the three new members of the set do provide a few voice-parts hitherto unknown; for example in Orlando Gibbons' 'Psalm cxlv', where the editors of *Tudor Church Music* have had to rest content with supplying by analogy three missing parts, two of which (Medius Decani and Contratenor I Cantoris) are now available at Peterhouse, and demonstrate how the composer intended the chord of the empty fifth at the end of his verses, instead of the Tierce de Picardie which is supplied in *Tudor Church Music*. The sphere in which these three volumes, probably unique in places, might be of greatest value is in the preparation of an edition of the works of Adrian Batten, whose music is scored in them, as in the other volumes of both sets, liberally.

COLLEGE MUSIC IN COSIN'S TIME

The general account of the Peterhouse part-books just given will already have suggested to the reader's mind some picture of a fertile and energetic revival of the 'Cathedral service' in the College chapel. But this movement was short-lived, for there is no evidence that it antedated the arrival of Cosin and the building of the chapel, and it ceased in 1642/3. This is hardly the place to insert a detailed summary of the Laudian revival and its influence upon the Universities and their colleges in general and Peterhouse in particular, but a few words may be included by way of helping to outline the scene.

The adventures of John Cosin in his earlier days as a vigorous young prebendary of Durham (1624–34) are well known, chiefly from the vivacity of Smart's language in his attacks. Suffice it to say that he returned to Cambridge equipped for the work of liturgical revival in music as well as in liturgy: music in those days was an essential part of a liberal education, not a matter of specialism or temperamental bent as it is with us. In these choir-books we see the High Church revival of the reign of Charles I translated into terms of music. A careful and expert interpretation of the Book of Common Prayer is clearly the mainspring of inspiration for those who compiled the Caroline books and possibly acquired also the Henrician set. This is all very faithfully reflected in the ritualistic indices of the English sets, with their headings such as 'Ad Dominus vobiscum', 'Ad Officium Altaris', 'Ad S. Cenam Domini', and the like. And in two other directions we can see how the High Church tendencies make themselves apparent.

The first of these is in the provision of music not only for the Kyrie (i.e. the Responses to the Ten Commandments) and Creed, but also in six cases for the Sanctus and in four cases for the Gloria in Excelsis. Now by the end of the sixteenth century the older custom of singing the whole of the Communion office had apparently been given up in most places, and the only harmonized settings that have been preserved from the time of Elizabeth are those by Tallis in the Dorian mode, Heath, and two by Causton. Of these the last three were printed by Day in 1560, but otherwise (like Marbeck's unison setting of the reign of Edward VI) they might well have been lost, as they are not copied in the contemporary manuscript books, nor printed in the collections of Barnard (1641) and thereafter. This oblivion has actually overtaken a service written by Whyte for his degree at Cambridge in 1560, and all but the bass part of a five-part setting by Tallis. Causton has fortunately been revived in our own day.[1] According to the late Mr S. Royle Shore[2] no other settings were written, so far as our knowledge goes, before about 1628: but between that date and 1645 Royle Shore records four—two by Child, one by Amner and one by Adrian Batten. Two of these four, with the Tallis service, are in our Peterhouse books, with the addition of a setting by Hooper, which Royle Shore overlooked, a total which points to the Master's intention to revive the singing of the whole Communion service.

[1] The Cathedral Series, No. 3 (Novello, 1913).
[2] 'The Choral Eucharist since the Reformation' (*Cathedral Quarterly*, April 1913).

The second point of interest lies in the liberal provision of music with Latin words, and that not only for motets or anthems but also in the texts of the offices themselves. Te Deum is written eight times in Latin, on three occasions with Jubilate Deo added: there are four Latin settings of the Litany and one, by Wilson the college organist, of the Kyrie and Creed. Three of the Latin settings of Te Deum and all the Latin litanies are by local men. The inclusion of a complete 'unreformed' Latin mass by Taverner would have been a *trouvaille* indeed to the critics of Cosin, had they only known of its existence: but there is no suggestion that he was going so far as to prepare for the introduction of the traditional texts of the Missal at Latin Communion services, and the indices show that the Taverner mass was intended to be used as a source for Latin anthems. It is worth notice that Evensong has no Latin music whatsoever, and was evidently intended to be kept in English always, perhaps because it would be a less academic service, attended by a higher proportion of the unlearned.

Entirely consistent with these tendencies is the large number of settings for Proper Psalms, going beyond those appointed in the Prayer Book. A table of these is given with the Indices to this book, at p. 54. We might also notice the frequent use of Collects as words for anthems, together with what is revealed by the Latin prayer books mentioned below (p. 51).

These books illustrate, then, the scene of Peterhouse taking a leading part in the liturgical revival of Laudian days. Laud himself, and Juxon the bishop of London, perhaps each contributed an anthem to the collection, though the identification of 'Mr Laud' and 'Mr Juxon' with the two doctors is not entirely proven. The Fellows stood behind the Master, as the College books indicate. The Chapel accounts for 1634–9[1] specify a subscription of £200 from the Master and Fellows for a pneumatic organ and 'Libros Chorales', with items on the expenditure side of £140 for the organ and £40 for the 'Libros Chorales'. Master, Fellows, and Scholars gave continuous and regular subscriptions for the organ, organists, and music, and the conditions laid down for the four Fellowships and four Scholarships of the Parke Foundation (18 March 1636) say: 'That every one of the said Fellows and Schollers shall endeavour to acquire so much knowledge in Song as to be able to perform their Parts with others that sing divine service in the Chapel.' The Decretum of 29 October 1635

---

[1] Walker, *op. cit.* pp. 127–8.

forbade the admission of 'pauperes scholares' who were not capable (and exercised) in music. Finally a Presbyterian writer of the period[1] shows us how the condition of things at Peterhouse appeared to an opposition critic of the time:

> Instead of Aristotle's Organon
> Anthems and organs I did study on....
>
> I cousen'd Dr Cosin and ere long
> A Fellowship obtained for a song.

[1] U.L.C. Add. MSS. 5820, ff. 121-3.

CATALOGUE OF THE MANUSCRIPTS

1. THE HENRICIAN SET

These part-books are consistent with one another in the order of their items, and are presented in the actual sequence of the manuscripts, followed by dates and references to the composers in alphabetical order.

		MS. 40 Tr.	MS. 41 Med.	MS. 31 Ct.	MS. 32 Bass	T.C.M.[1]
Sancte Deus	Taverner		I	I	I	III, 139
O rex gloriose	Mason		I	I	I	
Ave Dei Patris filia	Taverner		2	2	2	III, 61
Stabat mater	Hunt		3	3^v	3	
Salve regina	Pygott		4	5^v	4^v	
O Maria Deo grata	Fayrfax		5^v	7^v	6	
Maria plena gratiae	Fayrfax		7	9^v	7^v	
Salve regina	Ludford	Ff. 1–12 of the Triplex book are missing	8	11	9	
Trium regum	Catcott		9^v	12^v	10	
Ave Maria	Mason		10^v	13^v	10^v	
Mariae virginis	Bramston	13	12	15^v	12^v	
Euge dicta	Norman	13^v	13	16^v	13	
Ave Mariae divae matris	Aston	15	14	18	14^v	X, 127
Ave Maria mater Dei	Hunt	16	15^v	19	16	
Missa Te Deum	Aston	16^v	16	20	16	X, 1
Terrenum sitiens	Edwards	20	19	23^v	19	
Sub tuam protectionem	Northbroke	21	20	22^v	20	
Vae nobis miseris	Mason	21^v	20^v	25	20^v	
Quales sumus	Mason	23	21^v	26^v	21^v	
Gaude virgo mater Christi	Alen	24^v	23	28	23	
Missa (sine nomine)	Taverner	25	23^v	29	24	I, 50
Missa Mater Christi	Taverner	27^v	25^v	31^v	26	I, 99
Exsultet in hac die	Sturmys	30^v	28^v	34^v	29	
Sancte Deus	Whitbroke	31	29	35	29^v	
Ave Dei Patris filia	Fayrfax	31^v	29^v	36	30	
Missa Spes nostra	Jones	32^v	31	37	31	

Folios 36^v and 37 of the Triplex Book have been stuck down, presumably on purpose and at the time of writing, as the contents do not appear in the other books. The portion at the head of the page which is open reveals, however, that the copyist began to write in the *Te Deum* mass of Aston which occurs 20 folios further back, under the title of *Te matrem*—a paraphrastic text which alternates with the original words in the various MSS. of Aston's polyphonic setting of the hymn (see *Tudor Church Music*, x, 18 for details, and x, 7, top line, for a comparison with f. 37). The mistake would very soon have been found out, as the same music had been so recently inscribed: the test passage, 'qui sedes ad dexteram', is on the fifth and sixth lines of f. 17 in the Triplex book.

Missa Christe Jesu	Rasar	37^v	34^v	41	34	
Missa O quam glorifica	Fayrfax	40^v	38	45	37	
Missa Tecum principium	Fayrfax	45^v	42	50	41	

		MS. 40 Tr.	MS. 41 Med.	MS. 31 Ct.	MS. 32 Bass	T.C.M.[1]
Missa Albanus	Fayrfax	49	46	54ᵛ	44	
Missa Veni Sancte Spiritus	Pygott	52ᵛ	49ᵛ	59	47ᵛ	
Vidi aquam	(? Ludford)	56ᵛ	53ᵛ	64	51ᵛ	
Missa Christi Virgo	Ludford	57ᵛ	54ᵛ	65	52	
Salve intemerata	Tallis	61	57ᵛ	68	55	VI, 144
Mater Christi	Taverner	63	59ᵛ	70	56ᵛ	III, 92
O Christe pastor bone	Taverner	63ᵛ	60ᵛ	71	57	III, 73[2]
Gaude plurimum	Taverner	64	61	71	57ᵛ	III, 78
Missa Small Devotion[3]	Taverner	65ᵛ	62ᵛ	73	59	I, 70
Magnificat	Taverner	68ᵛ	65	76	61	III, 9
Magnificat	Dark	69	66	77	62	
Aspice Domine	Lupus Italus	70	67	78	63	
Missa (Surrexit pastor)	Lupus Italus	70ᵛ	67ᵛ	78ᵛ	63ᵛ	
Missa (sine nomine)	Tye	74	71	82	66ᵛ	
Sancta Maria mater	Pasche	76ᵛ	74	85	69	
Ave Dei Patris filia	Marbeck	78	74ᵛ	86	70	X, 215[4]
Magnificat	Appelby	79ᵛ	76	87	71ᵛ	
Missa (sine nomine)	(?)	80ᵛ	77ᵛ	89	72ᵛ	
Salve intemerata	Tallis	84	78ᵛ	92ᵛ	75ᵛ	VI, 144
Domine Jesu Christe	Ludford	85	78bᵛ	94ᵛ	77	
Magnificat	Jones	87	78cᵛ	96	78	
Magnificat	Pasche	88	79ᵛ	97	78ᵛ	
Magnificat (Regali)	Fayrfax	89	80ᵛ	98ᵛ	78bᵛ	
Aeterne laudis lilium	Fayrfax	89ᵛ	81	100ᵛ	79	
Magnificat (O bone Jesu)	Fayrfax	91	82	101ᵛ	79b	
Lauda vivi Alpha et O	Fayrfax	92	83	102ᵛ	79bᵛ	
Ave cujus conceptio	Ludford	93	84ᵛ	104	80	
Ave Maria ancilla	Ludford	94	85ᵛ	105	81	
Missa (O bone Jesu)	Fayrfax	95ᵛ	86ᵛ	106ᵛ	82	
Missa Inclina Domine	Ludford	98ᵛ	90	110	85	
Ave gratia plena Maria	Chamberlayne	102	93ᵛ	113ᵛ	87ᵛ	
Missa Salve intemerata	Tallis	103ᵛ	95	115	89	VI, 3
Missa Regnum mundi	Ludford	106	97	118	91ᵛ	
Fac nobis Domine	Taverner		101	121ᵛ	94	III, 135
Sub tuum praesidium	Taverner		102	122ᵛ	95	III, 141
Ave rosa sine spina	Tallis		102	122ᵛ	95	VI, 169
Ave Maria ancilla	Aston		103	123ᵛ	96ᵛ	X, 114
O baptista	Aston		104ᵛ	125	97ᵛ	X, 138
Gaude virgo mater Christi	Aston		106	127	99ᵛ	X, 85
Ave vulnus lateris	Erley		107ᵛ	128	100ᵛ	
Totius mundi domina	Martin		108ᵛ	129	101	
Missa Libera nos	Knight		111	131	103	

(In the MS. 40 Tr. column, spanning the last rows: "Ludford's Regnum mundi ends at 'lumen de lumine' in the Triplex. Credo: the rest of the Credo is missing")

[1] The Latin works of Aston, Marbeck, Tallis, and Taverner are printed in the *Tudor Church Music* folio edition: the references here are to volume and page.

[2] Under the title 'Jesu Christe pastor bone'.

[3] Dr E. H. Fellowes, in the Appendix to *Tudor Church Music* (1948) says: '*In all devotion* is probably the correct title. Dr John Jebb gave it this title in an unpublished treatise, now at Tenbury (Tenbury MS. 1239, p. 68), having so read the title in one of the early Peterhouse MS. part-books.' With Dr Jebb's proposal I am unable to agree, for in all four books the word 'Small' seems to be incontestable. It might be better to explain it as a secular theme from a song-title, on the analogy of the 'Western Wynde' used for a like purpose by Taverner, Sheppard, and Tye.

[4] Printed in *Tudor Church Music* without the tenor.

NOTES ON THE COMPOSERS IN THE HENRICIAN PART-BOOKS

Where up-to-date and trustworthy information is to be found in standard works, reference is made to them below: such details as are given here will be more usefully confined to the more obscure composers, several of whom are quite unknown except for their contributions to the Peterhouse part-books. 'Grove' indicates the fifth edition of Grove's *Dictionary of Music and Musicians*, edited by Eric Blom.

Transcripts of all the contents of the Henrician part-books by the late Alexander Ramsbotham are among the Tudor Church Music materials deposited in the Library of the University of London.

ALEN (Allen), William. Nothing further is known of this composer.

APPLEBY (Appelby), Thomas. Born in 1492[1]: organist at Lincoln Cathedral in 1536: at Magdalen College, Oxford, from 1539 to 1541, when he returned to Lincoln. He died in 1562 or 1563 and was succeeded by William Byrd (see Grove).

Jebb assigned the mass on ff. 80[v], 77[v], 89, 72[v] to Appleby, on the insufficient grounds that the preceding Magnificat is by him. His assumption was followed without due caution by some other writers, such as Jeffrey Mark[2] and Grattan Flood.[3] The mass should remain, unless and until identified, as anonymous. There is a different mass by Appleby, described as 'For a Mene', in the British Museum MSS. Addit. 17802-5.

ASTON, Hugh. See Grove, and *Tudor Church Music*, vol. X (1929). But note that the editors of this last are probably wrong in trying to identify him (following Henry Davey[4]) as the archdeacon of York whose will was proved in March 1523. It is much more likely that (as Jeffrey Mark,[5] Pulver,[6] and Grattan Flood[7] hold) he was the Canon of St Stephen's, Westminster, whose will was proved in December 1522.

BRAMSTON, Richard. One of the 'Practicioners' mentioned in the list given by Thomas Morley in his *Plain and Easie Introduction to Practicall Musicke* (1597; 2nd edn. 1608; 3rd edn. 1771). He was a chorister of Wells in 1485, deputy organist in 1507, probably succeeding to the regular post later, and was still living at Wells in 1550 as Keeper of the

---

[1] Aigrain, *Religious Music*, p. 176.
[2] In Grove, 2nd ed. 1915, also 3rd and 4th eds.
[3] In *Early Tudor Composers*, 1925.
[4] *A History of English Music*, 2nd ed. 1921, p. 105.
[5] In Grove.
[6] In *A Biographical Dictionary of Old English Musicians*.
[7] *Op. cit.*

Fabric.[1] The only other work known by him is a fine motet *Recordare Domine testamenti* in the British Museum MSS. Addit. 17802–5.[2]

CATCOTT. Jebb misread the title of Catcott's motet as *Trinum regnum*. No further facts have come to light either for Catcott or for the next four contributors:

CHAMBERLAYNE, Arthur,

DARK, John,

EDWARDS (unless this motet is an early work of the celebrated madrigalist Richard Edwardes, 1522–66), and

ERLEY (Erly, Erell), Walter. The copyist spells this name differently in the various books.

FAYRFAX, Robert (?1464–1521). Anthony à Wood describes him as 'the prime musitian of the nation'. See Grove: *Music and Letters*, vol. XXX (1949), p. 118: and *Musica Disciplina*, vol. VI (1952), p. 83.

HUNT, R. The only other known reference to this composer is the entry of the title of his *Stabat mater* in the fragment of an index on parchment in the binding of De Riminaldis, *Conciliorum* (Lyons, 1558), vol. II, in the library of Merton College, Oxford (Printed Book 62 f. 8).

JONES, Robert (*c.* 1485–1535 or later). He is mentioned as a Gentleman of the Chapel Royal in 1512 and 1526 and was at the Field of the Cloth of Gold in 1520 (Grove). His mass *Spes nostra* is to be found also in the British Museum MS. Addit. 34191, f. 1, but in the bass part only, which is itself imperfect at the beginning. The British Museum catalogue lists this, as in the case of Pygott's mass *Veni Sancte Spiritus*, incorrectly as a tenor part. The bass part of a 'three-men's song', 'Who shall have my fayr lady', is in the British Museum Printed Book K.1, e.1, usually known as the 'Wynkyn de Worde Song-book'.

KNIGHT, Robert. Organist of Salisbury Cathedral, 1530–40. In the Caroline set there is a motet by him, and in the British Museum MSS. Addit. 17802–5 are two more, with a Kyrie.

LUDFORD, Nicholas (? *c.* 1480–? 1542). See Grove. The anonymous 'Vidi aquam' which immediately precedes his mass *Christi Virgo* may be by the same composer, as the text is that of the Easter form for the holy-water ceremony just before the Sunday mass. Anonymity is so rare a feature in these part-books, the mass formerly ascribed to Appleby being the only other case, that the supposition is therefore quite probable.

LUPUS ITALUS. Ambrose Lupo of Milan, who was admitted as a 'Viall' in the King's band in 1540, died in 1594 or 1596, but his dates are not too late to make it possible that he was the Lupus Italus of the Peterhouse part-books. There was quite a dynasty of

---

[1] Aigrain, *op. cit.* p. 174.   [2] See Flood, *op. cit.*

the Lupo family in English Tudor music, seven of them being employed in the royal service (see Grove). This Mass has no title: it uses the Kyrie trope 'Surrexit pastor'.

MARBECK, John. See Grove, and *Tudor Church Music*, vol. X (1929).

MARTYN, Edward. Nothing is known of this composer.

MASON, John. He is described here as being of Chichester ('Cicerstiensis'). Morley includes 'Sir John Mason' among his 'Practicioners', and a musician of this name graduated Bachelor of Music at Oxford in 1508.

NORMAN, John. Two other compositions are ascribed to Norman, a mass *Resurrexit Dominus* at Oxford (Bodleian, MSS. Mus. Sch. e 376–81) and a motet *Miserere mei Domine* in the British Museum MS. Addit. 5665.

NORTHBROKE, James. Nothing is known of this composer, except that he proceeded Mus.Bac. at Oxford in 1531.[1]

PASHE (Pasche), William (*d.* 1525). There is a complete mass by him, *Christus resurgens*, in Caius College MS. 667, the countertenor and bass being also in the two part-books surviving in the University Library (MS. Dd xiii 27) and St John's College (MS. 234) respectively. Pulver[2] proposes that the 'Salve regina' signed 'W.P.' in the British Museum MS. Addit. 5665 should be attributed to Pashe, but it might equally well belong to W. Parsons (as the British Museum catalogue suggests), to Prentes, Proweth, or anyone else of the period who happened to have these initials. Pashe is in Morley's list of eminent musicians.

PYGOTT, Richard (? 1485–? 1552). Also in Morley's list. The medius part of his 'Salve regina' is also to be found in the British Museum MS. Harley 1709, and the bass of the mass *Veni Sancte Spiritus*, together with the bass of a lost motet, *Gaude pastore*, is in the same library (MS. Addit. 34191). In MS. Addit. 31922 is a sacred song for four voices, mostly in English, beginning 'Quid petis o filii'. The bass of a carol, 'By by', is in the so-called Wynkyn de Worde Song-book.

RASAR, William. This name was misread by Jebb, following Burney, as Kasar. The mass in these part-books is the only composition known by him: it is also to be found (complete) at Oxford, Bodleian Library, MSS. Mus. Sch. e 376–80.

STURMYS (Sturmes), Hugh. Nothing is known of this composer.

TALLIS, Thomas (*c.* 1505–85). See Grove, *Tudor Church Music*, vol. VI (1928); and the *Listener* (24 November 1949), p. 924.

TAVERNER, John (*c.* 1490–1545). See Grove; *Tudor Church Music*, vols. I and III (1923); and the *Listener* (10 February 1949), p. 244.

TYE, Christopher (*c.* 1497–1573). See Grove.

WHITBROKE, William (? *c.* 1495–?1560). See Grove.

---

[1] Anthony à Wood, *Fasti Oxonienses*. [2] In *Dictionary of Old English Musicians*.

2. THE CAROLINE PART-BOOKS

Unlike the Henrician books, the two English sets are paged in such a way that frequently they do not correspond with one another: furthermore there is of course no identity of arrangement between the Former and Latter sets. It will therefore be far better to abandon any attempt to catalogue the music in the order given, as no one of the fourteen books is entirely adequate as a standard; and to do what Jebb very wisely did in 1856, setting out the composers in alphabetical order. Their dates if known, and short details or references, can be given once and for all after each name.

As to the paging or foliation, only the Former set and the Medius Cantoris of the Latter set are numbered, the rest of the Latter set (and some pages of the Medius Cantoris as well) being thus arranged—we quote from Jebb's manuscript Catalogue:

The order of the alphabet is employed, often followed by numerals, as A, A1, A2, etc. It often happens, however, that some unnumbered leaves occur, as, for example, between A3 and A4: or the same letters and numbers are employed for several consecutive leaves, as B3, B3, B3. To remedy this confusion it has been thought advisable, in this Index, to mark these unnumbered leaves by figures within brackets, as B3(1), B3(2) and so on.

Jebb's solution of the difficulty is practical, and it does not seem possible to improve upon it. It has been followed in the references given in the *Tudor Church Music* volumes for Byrd, Gibbons, Tallis, Taverner, Tomkins, and White, which is an adequate reason for retaining it in the present compilation. There may be those who will regret the decision and think that the Latter set, together with the Organ Book, which has neither page nor folio numbering, should at this juncture and for the purpose of this catalogue be re-foliated throughout. But the disadvantages of such a scheme would be that the possibility of checking so much of the music from the classical edition of *Tudor Church Music* would disappear.

References in square brackets such as [Ely], [Glouc.], and so on refer to laborious comparisons made by Jebb—sometimes with the result of a successful identification of an otherwise anonymous composition—with manuscript part-books existing elsewhere. That they are printed in square brackets indicates

7

that they have not been verified for the purposes of the present volume, though it is not intended thereby to cast any reflection upon the accuracy and care with which Jebb carried out this portion of his labours. Where he failed not infrequently was (apparently) in the task of deciphering his own manuscript notes of folio numbers: thus when upon examination of the original his 'S4' turns out to be '54' we can see that the failing was in calligraphy rather than in musicology.

Search in the published works of Byrd, Tallis, White, and others, and in the catalogues of the British Museum, Christ Church, Oxford, and elsewhere has failed to provide any clues to the authorship of the anonymous pieces. The set of Latin motet parts (bass) in the fly-leaves of MS. 37 (Bass Decani, Latter set) is peculiarly interesting and exasperating. They give the impression of being first-class polyphonic work of the style of Dering or Philips, but with one exception (Philips, *Aspice Domine quia facta*) they have not been traced as yet, and they are not among the many printed works of Dering and Philips in the British Museum. Some of them are marked '8 voc'.

The ordinary contractions are used for portions of the Prayer-Book Services: Ven. (Venite), TD (Te Deum), Bdte (Benedicite), Btus (Benedictus), Jub. (Jubilate), Lit. (Litany), Ky. (Kyrie, the title used throughout for the responses to the Ten Commandments), Cr. (Creed), Stus (Sanctus), Gl. (Gloria in excelsis), Mag. (Magnificat), and Nd. (Nunc dimittis).

The references in the centre column are as follows:

BARN.: John Barnard's *First Book of Selected Church Musick* (1641). Ten parts (five each for Decani and Cantoris). Excessively scarce, the only complete set being now at Christ Church, Oxford. See Grove.

BATT.: Adrian Batten's Organ Book, now at St Michael's College, Tenbury, MS. 791.

BOYCE: William Boyce's *Cathedral Music*, 3 vols. (1760–78).

[ELY]: manuscripts in Ely Cathedral Library, not further particularized by Jebb. See further W. E. Dickson, *Catalogue of Ancient Choral Services...in the Cathedral of Ely* (1861).

[GLOUC.]: manuscripts in the Contratenor Secundus part-book of Barnard, at Gloucester Cathedral.

JEBB: John Jebb's *Choral Responses and Litanies of the United Church of England and Ireland*, 2 vols. (1847–57).

[LAMB.]: manuscript part-book (bass) in Lambeth Palace Library, erroneously lettered 'Services and Anthems by Thomas Morley'.

[HEREF.]: manuscripts in the Hereford Cathedral copies of Barnard, which have been transferred in the present century to Christ Church, Oxford.

[LICH.]: manuscripts in the copies of Barnard at Lichfield Cathedral.

[ST JOHN'S]: manuscript part-book in the library of St John's College, Oxford.

TUD.: six volumes written by Thomas Tudway between 1715 and 1720: British Museum, Harley MSS. 7337–42.

The entries marked '*Organ-Book* 1' refer to the numbers of the items in the Organ Book, MS. 46.

| LATTER SET | | | | | | | COMPOSER, TITLE AND REFERENCES | FORMER SET | | | | | | |
| CANTORIS | | | DECANI | | | | | CANTORIS | | | DECANI | | | |
MS. 36 B	MS. 43 T	MS.45 Med.	MS. 37 B	MS. 35 T	MS. 42 CT	MS. 44 Med.		MS. 33 B	CTI	MS. 34 Med.	MS. 38 B	CTII	MS. 39 CTI	Med.
							AMNER, John. *Mus.Bac. Oxon.* 1613, *Can-tab.* 1640. *Organist of Ely,* 1610–41. *d.* 1641							
R2	Q2	105	P3	V5	P6	R6	First Preces and Psalms for Christmas Day, Evensong¹							
R2(2)ᵛ	Q2(2)ᵛ	106ᵛ	P4ᵛ	V6ᵛ	P6(2)ᵛ	R6	Second Preces and Venite²							
							'Caesar's' Service in G:³ Ven, TD, Jub, Ky., Cr., Mag., Nd. [Ely], Tud.	48	45ᵛ	44ᵛ	57		49ᵛ	47
							Service in D mi.: TD, Btus, Ky., Cr., Gl., Mag., Nd.⁴ *Organ-Book* I (*Gloria only*), [Ely]	84	80	83	90		92	84
							A stranger here⁵ Tud.		141ᵛ	152			164ᵛ	
R3	Q3	107	P1	W1	Q1	S1	Hear O Lord							155
							How⁶ doth the city⁵	151	141⁷				164	
Q5ᵛ	P6ᵛ	103ᵛ	O10ᵛ	V1ᵛ	P2ᵛ	R2	I will sing unto the Lord⁵							
							Lift up your heads	84(2)		84			92(2)	85
							Lord I am not high-minded [Ely]				89	51	90	83

¹ Q2(3) of MS. 43 has the Minister's part.
² Q2(4ᵛ) of MS. 43 has the Minister's part.
³ For Dr Henry Caesar, Dean of Ely, 1616–36.
⁴ In the Folio Prayer-Book (see p. 49 below) is also the alto part of a Sursum corda and Sanctus.
⁵ Printed in Amner's *Sacred Hymns of 3, 4, 5 and 6 parts, for Voices and Vyols* (1615).
⁶ Written in every case as 'Now doth the city'.
⁷ Music not filled in.

| FORMER SET | | | | | | | COMPOSER, TITLE AND REFERENCES | LATTER SET | | | | | | |
| CANTORIS | | | DECANI | | | | | DECANI | | | | CANTORIS | | |
MS. 33 B	— CTI	MS. 34 Med.	MS. 38 B	— CTII	MS. 39 CTI	— Med.		MS. 44 Med.	MS. 42 CT	MS. 35 T	MS. 37 B	MS. 45 Med.	MS. 43 T	MS. 36 B
							O come hither and hearken	R5	P5	V4	P2	104		
							O sing unto the Lord [Ely]	R4	P4	V3	O12		Q1(2)	R1
							O ye little flock¹	R3	P3	V2	O11		Q1	Q6
			88		91	82	Out of the deep (for 3 voices)							
	140ᵛ		163		164	154ᵛ	Remember not¹							
150ᵛ		151ᵛ	162ᵛ²			154ᵛ	Woe is me¹							
							BATTEN, Adrian. *Vicar-choral of Westminster Abbey, 1614. Organist of St Paul's from 1624. d. 1637 or 1640*							
							Fourth Evening Service in D mi.: Mag., Nd.	D3	G1	F5	F3	23	F5	G4
							Litany and Suffrages	A4	5ᵛ	B4ᵛ	A4ᵛ			A4ᵛ
							Blessed are all those				G5			G5ᵛ
111ᵛ	108	110ᵛ	118ᵛ	69	120ᵛ	115ᵛ	Christ rising again							

¹ Printed in Amner's *Sacred Hymns of 3, 4, 5 and 6 parts, for Voices and Vyols* (1615).   ² Music not filled in.

FORMER SET							COMPOSER, TITLE AND REFERENCES	LATTER SET						
DECANI				CANTORIS				DECANI				CANTORIS		
— Med.	MS. 39 CT I	— CT II	MS. 38 B	MS. 34 Med.	— CT I	MS. 33 B		MS. 44 Med.	MS. 42 CT	MS. 35 T	MS. 37 B	MS. 45 Med.	MS. 43 T	MS. 36 B
							BATTEN, Adrian (*continued*)							
138	148v			134v	128v		Deliver us O Lord *Boyce*	U5v	S3v	R5	H2 R5		K4 U2	K6v T9
125	131	76	131	124	117	125	Have mercy upon me O God *Organ-Book 5*							
134	145	85	141	139		135	Hear my prayer O God *Boyce*				G5v			
							Hear my prayer O Lord				G6v			G6v
74 116 133	81v 82 123 144	60v 84	119v 140	74 114 138	71v 72 108v	74v 114 134	Holy, holy, holy (for Trinity Sunday)							
							The music on ff. 83, 72 of the Contratenor books is the Contratenor Secundus. The two parts being on the left and right of one opening make it clear that the books were shared by two singers on each side of the choir. More important is the evidence supplied by the non-appearance of this second contratenor part when the anthem is written in later, at f. 108v of the Contratenor Cantoris, which places it beyond reasonable doubt that a Contratenor Secundus book was also once in existence for Cantoris as well as for Decani. The Tenor Cantoris part is in the British Museum, MSS. Addit. 30478 and 30479.							
117	124	67v	121	115	110v	115	I heard a voice							
116v	122v	67	120	113v	109	113v	Jesus said unto Peter							
133v	144v	84v	140v	138v	134v	134v	O how happy a thing it is							

COMPOSER, TITLE AND REFERENCES	FORMER SET							LATTER SET						
	DECANI				CANTORIS			DECANI				CANTORIS		
	Med.	MS. 39 CTI	CTII	MS. 38 B	MS. 34 Med.	CTI	MS. 33 B	MS. 44 Med.	MS. 42 CT	MS. 35 T	MS. 37 B	MS. 45 Med.	MS. 43 T	MS. 36 B
O Lord let me know mine end *Organ-Book 4*		133			125	118^v	128	G6						
O Lord thou hast searched me out [Lich.], Batt.								F5	H4	H6	K2	40	I5	N4
Out of the deep *Barn.*								G1	H5	I6	G6 L3			
Ponder my words *Organ-Book 11*								E5	H2	H3	G5 I3	38	I3	M5
Praise the Lord O my soul *Organ-Book 12*								E6	H3	H4	I4	39	I4	M6
Turn thou us	113	123^v	68	116	114^v	107	114^v							
BECK, Anthony. *Precentor of Norwich*														
Who can tell how oft he offendeth								G7^v	G9^v	H7^v	G8^1 G9^v		G7	K7
BENNET, John. *c. 1570–1615*														
O God of gods^2 [Lamb.]	135^v	146^v			135	126^v	123^v							

[1] The voice-part at G8 is marked 'Secundus'.
[2] Also in British Museum, MSS. Addit. 29372–6, and Sacred Harmonic Society MS. 1642: and Christ Church, Oxford, MSS. 56–60 (lacking bass) with Organ part in

MS. 67. This is the only anthem known from the famous madrigalist; it is for five voices and instruments.

FORMER SET								LATTER SET						
DECANI				CANTORIS			COMPOSER, TITLE AND REFERENCES	DECANI				CANTORIS		
— Med.	MS.39 CTI	— CTII	MS.38 B	MS.33 B	— CTI	MS.34 Med.		MS.44 Med.	MS.42 CT	MS.35 T	MS.37 B	MS.45 Med.	MS.43 T	MS.36 B
							BLANCKE, J.							
39^v	54	36	43	41	38	37^v	Evening Service: Mag., Nd.							
							BOYCE, Thomas. *Mus.Bac. Oxon.* 1603							
57	65^v		63^v	63	57	57	Short Service: TD, Btus, Ky., Cr., Mag., Nd. [Lich.]							
							Te Deum (Latin)	K11	K5(8)		F11	66		H1(5)
							BULL, John. 1562–1628							
111	119 154^v[2]	70	114^v	109	105^v	109	Almighty God, who by the leading of a star[1]							
							BYRD, William. 1543–1623							
						99^v	First Preces[3]		L3(2)^v	A3^v				
23	27	25	28	24	23	23	Second Preces and Psalms for the Epiphany							
24	28	26	29	25	24	24	Second Preces and Psalm for Ascension Day, Evensong[4]							

[1] The Collect for the Epiphany: known as 'The Starr Anthem'. Printed in *Tudor Church Music*, octavo series, no. 91, ed. E. H. Fellowes.
[2] The opening portion only; words without music supplied to the end.
[3] The naming and order of the Preces follows that in vol. II of *Tudor Church Music* (1922) in which all Byrd's English Church music is printed.
[4] Ps. xxiv is an adaptation of his 'Attollite portas' (*Tudor Church Music*, II, xxxi).

Grouping of columns — FORMER SET: DECANI (Med., MS. 39 CTI, CTII, MS. 38 B) and CANTORIS (MS. 34 Med., CTI, MS. 33 B). LATTER SET: DECANI (MS. 44 Med., MS. 42 CT, MS. 35 T, MS. 37 B) and CANTORIS (MS. 45 Med., MS. 43 T, MS. 36 B).

Med.	MS. 39 CTI	CTII	MS. 38 B	MS. 34 Med.	CTI	MS. 33 B	COMPOSER, TITLE AND REFERENCES	MS. 44 Med.	MS. 42 CT	MS. 35 T	MS. 37 B	MS. 45 Med.	MS. 43 T	MS. 36 B
							(Third) Preces and Responses							
							Short Service: TD,Btus,Ky.,[1] Cr.,[1] Mag.,Nd.	C4v	B3	C5	A5	A4	A1	B6 I4
							Ky., Cr.	M3	N1	T1	E1	6 / 93v	C4	
						159v	Ky. (alternative version)	Q2	O1v	Q1	O1[2]		N5	P3
							Mag., Nd.	B2	B1	B6	A3			
							Te Deum (Latin version)	C3	D6	E5	C5	65	R4	H1(4)
77	85	47	84 / 106v	77 / 99v	75	79	Great Service: Mag., Nd. *Organ-Book* 19	K10	K5(7)	A3v (Magnificat) / B1 (Nunc dimittis)	F10			
	17		14[4]	15			Service in F ("4 voc. full") TD, Btus[3] [Lamb.]		L3v					
139	150		142				Behold I bring you glad tidings[5]							
							Fac cum servo tuo[6]	O5v		P5v	M6v	69v		M6v
							How long O Lord	G3v	D2	A2			A2	

[1] The 'alternative' Kyrie and Creed as given in *Tudor Church Music.*

[2] 'Mr Bird, Kyrie & Credo to his Great Service. This is ye Right Creed.' This confident statement is not borne out by the *Tudor Church Music* edition.

[3] These are the only fragments known of this Service in F. Cf. E. H. Fellowes, *William Byrd* (2nd ed. 1948), pp. 130, 131. But Jebb notes that the bass part is also at Lambeth.

[4] No music, and only part of the words of Te Deum.

[5] Adapted from his 'Ne irascaris' (*Cantiones Sacrae*, 1589, I, 20) and so headed in the Bass Decani book.

[6] *Cantiones Sacrae*, II, 5.

	LATTER SET							FORMER SET						
	CANTORIS			DECANI				COMPOSER, TITLE AND REFERENCES	CANTORIS			DECANI			
	MS. 36 B	MS. 43 T	MS. 45 Med.	MS. 37 B	MS. 35 T	MS. 42 CT	MS. 44 Med.		MS. 33 B	CTI	MS. 34 Med.	MS. 38 B	CTII	MS. 39 CTI	Med.
BYRD, William (*continued*)															
Lætentur cœli[1]	M6		69	M6			O5	Lætentur cœli[1]							
O God the proud are risen — *Organ-Book 26*								O God the proud are risen — *Organ-Book 26*	106ᵛ		104ᵛ	110ᵛ		113ᵛ	106ᵛ
O Lord give ear — *Organ-Book 33*								O Lord give ear — *Organ-Book 33*	78ᵛ	74	76ᵛ	83ᵛ	46	84ᵛ	76ᵛ
O Lord make thy servant Charles — *Organ-Book 24*	G6						H2	O Lord make thy servant Charles — *Organ-Book 24*			106	112		115	108
Prevent us O Lord	Q5	P6	103	O10	V1	P2	R2	Prevent us O Lord							
Sing joyfully unto God — *Organ-Book 25*								Sing joyfully unto God — *Organ-Book 25*	106		104	110		113	106
CHILD, William. 1606-97															
'Sharp Service' (D ma.): Ven., TD, Jub., Ky., Cr., Mag., Nd. — Boyce (without Venite)								'Sharp Service' (D ma.): Ven., TD, Jub., Ky., Cr., Mag., Nd. — Boyce (without Venite)	7	8	7ᵛ	7ᵛ		7ᵛ	7ᵛ
Service in G ma.: Bte, Jub, Ky., Cr., Mag., Nd.								Service in G ma.: Bte, Jub, Ky., Cr., Mag., Nd.	70	67	70	75		77	70
Sanctus and Gloria (8 voices)								Sanctus and Gloria (8 voices)	137	132ᵛ	140ᵛ	143ᵛ		152	141

¹ *Cantiones Sacrae*, I, 28.

	FORMER SET DECANI				FORMER SET CANTORIS			COMPOSER, TITLE AND REFERENCES	LATTER SET DECANI				LATTER SET CANTORIS		
	— Med.	MS. 39 CTI	— CTII	MS. 38 B	MS. 34 Med.	— CTI	MS. 33 B		MS. 44 Med.	MS. 42 CT	MS. 35 T	MS. 37 B	MS. 45 Med.	MS. 43 T	MS. 36 B
								Latin Te Deum and Jubilate[1]	K6	K5(3)	H1(3)	F12	60	N3(3)	G5(2)
								Burial Service	H5	E4	I2	O4	31	H6	O4
	143v	156(2)v		147	143	135	139v	Collect for All Saints							
	144	156v		147v	143v			Bow down thine ear	I2(2)			L6		K6	
							140	Give the king thy judgements			I4				
								Hear O my people	G7		H7	G8^{v2} Gg²	30	G7v	K7v
								O God wherefore art thou absent	I2	L1(4)	L3(2)	L5(2)			
	15	92v		89v	159	79v	84(2)v	O let my mouth be filled	H2(3)	K8(2)	H3(2)	H6	55	MI(2)	L8
	142	153		145v	141v	133	138	Sing we merrily — Boyce							
	145	157(2)v		148v	145	137	141	Turn thou us, good Lord							
								What shall I render	H2(2)	K8(3)	H3(3)	H5(2)	54	MI(3)	L7

[1] 'A morning Service in Lattin made for the Right worll Dr Cofin by Mr Child.' Cosin was Vice-Chancellor in 1639.

[2] 'Contratenor Decany' and 'Secundus Decany' respectively: on one opening so that two singers could share the book.

LATTER SET							COMPOSER, TITLE AND REFERENCES	FORMER SET						
CANTORIS			DECANI					CANTORIS			DECANI			
MS. 36 B	MS. 43 T	MS. 45 Med.	MS. 37 B	MS. 35 T	MS. 42 CT	MS. 44 Med.		MS. 33 B	— CTI	MS. 34 Med.	MS. 38 B	— CTII	MS. 39 CTI	— Med.
							CRANFORD, Thomas or William[1]							
							I will love thee O Lord [Heref., Lamb., Lich.], Batt.	156v		159v	170v		171v	
							O Lord make thy servant Charles	104	101	106v	112v		115v	108v
							DERING, Richard. c. 1580–1657							
							Collect for Easter Day[2]	75	72v	74v	79v	44	82v	74v
	K4(3)		I1	K8	L1(2)	O2(3)	Therefore with angels; and Sanctus							
	K4(2)		I2	K7	L2(3)	O2(2)	Lord thou art worthy							
							DERRICK							
K3	E6	20	G2	H5	K4	H4	Kyrie and Creed	82	78	80v	86v	49v	88	80v
				C1	B2	B3	Kyrie only							
A6	A6	4	C2	D3	C1	C1	Jubilate							

[1] More likely *Thomas*, who was one of the vicars-choral of St Pauls. See Myles B. Foster, *Anthems and Anthem-Composers* (1901), p. 31. William Cranford is said to have been born about 1635. But the Batten Organ-book at Tenbury names him William.

[2] Probably an adaptation from the Latin, as the repetitions of text at the end are grotesquely absurd for so talented a master as Dering. The same may be true of the other two anthems. In Mace's *Musick's Monument* (1676) it is said that Dering's compositions enjoyed great favour at Cambridge before the introduction of the 'scoulding violins'.

Table columns are grouped as follows. **LATTER SET** — *Cantoris*: MS. 36 B, MS. 43 T, MS. 45 Med.; *Decani*: MS. 37 B, MS. 35 T, MS. 42 CT, MS. 44 Med. **FORMER SET** — *Decani*: — Med., MS. 39 CTI, — CTII, MS. 38 B; *Cantoris*: MS. 34 Med., — CTI, MS. 33 B.

MS. 36 B	MS. 43 T	MS. 45 Med.	MS. 37 B	MS. 35 T	MS. 42 CT	MS. 44 Med.	COMPOSER, TITLE AND REFERENCES	— Med.	MS. 39 CTI	— CTII	MS. 38 B	MS. 34 Med.	— CTI	MS. 33 B
							ESTE, Michael. c. 1580–1648							
F1	L3	46	E4	K4	I2	I4	Evening Service: Mag., Nd. [Lich.]							
F2v	L4v	49	E6	L1	K1	K1	Awake and stand up							
F3	L5	48	E5	K6	I4	I6	Blow out the trumpet[1]							
F4	L6	49v	E6v	L2	K1v	K1v	O clap your hands together [Lich.]							
F5	M1	50v	E7v	L2v	K2v	·K2v	O Lord of whom I do depend							
							FARRANT, John. Organist of Ely, 1567–1572; of Salisbury, 1598. d. 1602							
F6			F2				Short Service: Ven, TD, Jub, Ky, Mag., Nd.[3]	55	63		62	55	55	61
							FARRANT, Richard. d. 1580							
I6	T3	96	E2		N3v[4]	M5	Service: TD, Btus, Ky., Cr., Mag., Nd.[3] [Glouc.], Boyce, Tud.							
							Call to remembrance	162			157v	148v		147

---

[1] Printed in Rimbault's *Anthems* (Musical Antiquarian Society, 1845).   [3] *Ibid.* no. 63 (TD, Btus) and no. 33 (Mag., Nd.), ed. E. H. Fellowes.

[2] *Tudor Church Music*, octavo series, no. 54 (TD, Jub., Mag., Nd.), ed. E. H. Fellowes.   [4] Ends half-way through Magnificat.

| FORMER SET | | | | | | | COMPOSER, TITLE AND REFERENCES | LATTER SET | | | | | | |
| DECANI | | | | CANTORIS | | | | DECANI | | | | CANTORIS | | |
— Med.	MS. 39 CTI	— CTII	MS. 38 B	MS. 34 Med.	— CTI	MS. 33 B		MS. 44 Med.	MS. 42 CT	MS. 35 T	MS. 37 B	MS. 45 Med.	MS. 43 T	MS. 36 B
							FERRABOSCO, Alfonso. *d.* 1588							
							Sanctus	P6v						
96v	106v		102v	95v	92v	96v	Have ye no regard [Lamb., Lich.], Batt.							
							FIDO, John. *Organist of Hereford,* 1593–4							
136v	147			133	127	124v	Hear me O Lord Batt.						K3	K5
							GEERES, John							
							Collect for St John's Day	I3	I1	K3	K1	45	L2	N3
							GIBBONS, Orlando. 1583–1625[1]							
							First Preces and Psalm cxlv. 15–21 (for Whitsunday)	B4	B4	C6	B2	A6	A4	A3
33v			38²	26	30		First Preces and Psalms lvii. 9–12, cxviii. 19–24 (for Easter Day, Evensong)							
5	5v		5v	5v	5v	4v	Second Preces and Psalm cxlv. 1–14 [presumably for Whitsunday, Evensong]							

---

[1] The English Church music of Gibbons is to be found in vol. IV of *Tudor Church Music* (1922).

[2] Wrongly entered to William Smith in the Peterhouse MS. Jebb did not notice this error, and it escaped the expert eyes of the editors of *Tudor Church Music*, only attracting the notice of the present compiler through its lonely appearance among the works of William Smith, which are otherwise present very completely. The item is of great value, as it gives us the missing part (or one of them) for 'Awake up my glory'. In the meantime, nine years after the publication of *Tudor Church Music* IV in 1925, Dr E. H. Fellowes found a similar part from Durham (see *Tudor Church Music: Appendix* (1948), pp. 11, 28).

COMPOSER, TITLE AND REFERENCES	FORMER SET DECANI — Med.	MS. 39 CTI	— CTII	MS. 38 B	FORMER SET CANTORIS MS. 34 Med.	— CTI	MS. 33 B	LATTER SET DECANI MS. 44 Med.	MS. 42 CT	MS. 35 T	MS. 37 B	LATTER SET CANTORIS MS. 45 Med.	MS. 43 T	MS. 36 B
Short Service: Venite								A1		N4	B8	A2	F3	A4
TD, Btus, Ky., Cr., Mag., Nd.									L5	R5	D1	86		
TD, Btus, Ky., Cr.													R4(2)	
TD, Btus, Mag., Nd.														
Ky.								B3v	B2v	C1v				H2
Mag., Nd.								L2				27	F6 R7	E2
Te Deum (Latin adaptation)								K12	K5(2)	H1(2)	F5	62	N3(4)	G5(4)
Te Deum (in Latin)										H1(7)				
Second Service: Mag., Nd.	95	105		101(3)	94	91	'95							
Behold I bring you glad tidings	110	118	59	114	108	105	108							
Behold thou hast made my days (1618)[1]	109	116v		113	107	101v	105							

[1] 'This Anthem was made at the entretie of Doctor Maxcie Deane of Winsor the same day sennight before his death'—Christ Church, Oxford, MS. 21, f. 272—quoted in *Tudor Church Music*, IV, xxxi.

FORMER SET — DECANI				FORMER SET — CANTORIS			COMPOSER, TITLE AND REFERENCES	LATTER SET — DECANI				LATTER SET — CANTORIS		
— Med.	MS. 39 CTI	— CTII	MS. 38 B	MS. 34 Med.	— CTI	MS. 33 B		MS. 44 Med.	MS. 42 CT	MS. 35 T	MS. 37 B	MS. 45 Med.	MS. 43 T	MS. 36 B
							GIBBONS, Orlando (continued)							
113v	163[1]		160				Glorious and powerful God	H1			B5	51	M2	
	120	68v	117	110	107v	110	If ye then be risen with Christ							
				131v			This is the record of John *Organ-Book 2*	A2[2] F6[3]	H1	H2	L1		I1v	
79v	87	49	86	79v	77	81	We praise thee O Father *Organ-Book 20*							
							GILES, Nathaniel. *c.* 1558–1633							
11v	13v		12v	11v	12	11v	Second Service: TD, Jub., Cr. Barn.	C5v						
93v	103v		99v	92v		93v	Mag., Nd. Barn.							
114v	122		118	113	109v	113	Collect for Whitsunday Batt.							
	139	60					Have mercy upon me O God Batt.				K6	29	H1	O2
							He that hath my commandments		G4v	G1v	I6v			N2

¹ Words only.   ² Solo part.   ³ Chorus.

| | FORMER SET | | | | | | | COMPOSER, TITLE AND REFERENCES | LATTER SET | | | | | | |
| | DECANI | | | | CANTORIS | | | | DECANI | | | | CANTORIS | | |
	— Med.	CTI MS. 39	CTII —	B MS. 38	Med. MS. 34	CTI —	B MS. 33		Med. MS. 44	CT MS. 42	T MS. 35	B MS. 37	Med. MS. 45	T MS. 43	B MS. 36
								O give thanks unto the Lord Barn.	G3	D1v	A1v				
		157		148	144v		140v	Out of the deep Batt.							
								HEATH, John. ? 1608–68. *Organist of Rochester*							
				24				Evening Service: Mag., Nd. Batt.	I	A1	I	A1	I	I	I
								HILTON, John (*the elder*). *d.* 1608							
	76	84	46	83	76	74v	78	Call to remembrance[1] Organ-Book 32							
								HILTON, John (*the younger*): 1599–1656/7							
	38			37	32		35v	Hear my cry O God Organ-Book 15							
	97	107		103	96	93v	97	Sweet Jesus [Lich.]							
								HINDE, Richard							
	153v	162		160v	150		145v	O sing unto the Lord (1632) Organ-Book 6, [Lich.]	G2	H6	I5	H5	4I	I6	L6

¹ *Tudor Church Music,* octavo series, no. 97, ed. E. H. Fellowes.

| FORMER SET | | | | | | | COMPOSER, TITLE AND REFERENCES | LATTER SET | | | | | | |
| DECANI | | | | CANTORIS | | | | DECANI | | | | CANTORIS | | |
— Med.	MS. 39 CTI	— CTII	MS. 38 B	MS. 34 Med.	— CTI	MS. 33 B		MS. 44 Med.	MS. 42 CT	MS. 35 T	MS. 37 B	MS. 45 Med.	MS. 43 T	MS. 36 B
							HOOPER, Edmund. *c.* 1553–1621 *Organist of Westminster Abbey,* 1606							
68	75	40	81	68	65	67	(First) Great Service: Mag., Nd. [Lamb.]							
99	109		105^{v}	98	96^{v}	99^{v}	(Second) Short Service: Mag., Nd.		$A3^{1}$	$A3^{1}$				
50^{v}	42^{2} / 58^{v}		52^{v}	49	49^{v}	44^{v}	(Third) Verse Service: Mag., Nd. Batt.							
							Sanctus and Gloria [Lamb.]		$D1^{3}$ / F1	O1	C1			
	137		130	123		122	Collect for Christmas Day *Organ-Book* 17							
110^{v}	118^{v}	59^{v}	114^{v}	108^{v}	105^{v}	108^{v}	Collect for the Circumcision							
107	114		111	105	107	107	Behold it is Christ *Organ-Book* 22, Barn.	G3	D1	A1		36	H5	
119	129	72	122	116	104	116	O God of gods						$K2^{v}$	
112	121	70^{v}	115^{v}	111^{v}	106^{v}	109^{v}	The Blessed Lamb							

[1] Nunc dimittis only.
[2] F. 42 is the first contratenor part, f. 58ᵛ the second.
[3] Marked Tallis, but by Hooper.

COMPOSER, TITLE AND REFERENCES	FORMER SET DECANI — Med.	MS. 39 CTI	— CTII	MS. 38 B	CANTORIS MS. 34 Med.	— CTI	MS. 33 B	LATTER SET DECANI MS. 44 Med.	MS. 42 CT	MS. 35 T	MS. 37 T	CANTORIS MS. 45 Med.	MS. 43 T	MS. 36 B
HUGHES														
Mag., Nd., 'to Derrick's Short Service'[1]	40v	44v 56v		44v	39	41	42							
HUTCHINSON, John. b. 1615														
Behold how good and joyful[2]								T6	Q6(2)v	X4	Q6v		S4	S5
HUTCHINSON, Richard. Organist of Durham. c. 1614–44. d. 1646														
Hear my crying								E2		G3	H3.	33	H3	L2
Lord I am not high-minded								D5			K5	21v 28	H2	O1
Of mortal men[3]								E3		G4v	H4	34	H4	L2
Ye that fear the Lord	127	138	77	133	127	122	129							
JEFFRIES, Matthew, of Wells. Mus.Bac. Oxon. 1593														
Rejoice in the Lord Organ-Book 34	130v	142v		137v						F2[4] H5v		20v	E6v	K3v

[1] Also at Durham.

[2] Jeffrey Mark, in *Grove's Dictionary of Music and Musicians* (1927) assigned this to Richard Hutchinson, but all six Peterhouse entries carefully name him John Hutchinson, whereas those ascribed here to Richard Hutchinson have the Christian name appended in only two out of twenty-five entries. 'Hear my crying' is ascribed in Bass Cantoris to 'Mr Huchinson of York'.

[3] Here called the 'Southwell Anthem'. The words are doleful and unchristian.

[4] The two tenor parts are different, and the anthem is described as being for six voices.

| LATTER SET | | | | | | | COMPOSER, TITLE AND REFERENCES | FORMER SET | | | | | | |
| CANTORIS | | | DECANI | | | | | CANTORIS | | | DECANI | | | |
MS. 36 B	MS. 43 T	MS.45 Med.	MS. 37 B	MS. 35 T	MS. 42 CT	MS. 44 Med.		MS. 33 B	— CTI	MS. 34 Med.	MS. 38 B	— CTII	MS. 39 CTI	— Med.
							JUXON, (?) William.[1] 1582–1663							
T1	S6	120	Q8	X6	R2	U2	Christ rising again *Batt.*							
							KNIGHT, Robert. *Organist of Salisbury, 1530–40*							
		70	N1	P6		O6	Propterea moestum							
							LAUD, (?) William.[1] 1573–1645							
P2(2)ᵛ	N5ᵛ	74ᵛ	O3	Q4	O2		Praise the Lord O my soul[2] *Tud.*							
							LOOSEMORE, Henry. *c. 1600–70. Organist of King's College, 1627. Mus.Bac. 1640*							
							First Service in D mi.: TD, Jub, Litany, Ky., Cr., Mag, Nd.			153ᵛ	167		167	155ᵛ
A2(2)	A3(2)	B1	A1	B3	A2(2)[3] D3ᵛ [4]	A6(2)	Latin Litany from the same Service							
							Second Service in G mi.: Bdte, Jub.			156ᵛ	168ᵛ [5]		169ᵛ	159
P6ᵛ	O2	76	N5	Q5ᵛ	O4(2)	Q3(2)	Latin Litany in G mi.							

[1] John S. Bumpus in his *History of English Cathedral Music* (p. 95, footnote) saw no reason against identifying these two names with the Bishop of London and the Archbishop of Canterbury respectively: though they are described in the MSS. merely as 'Mr Juxon' and 'Mr Laud'. Laud proceeded D.D. in 1608, Juxon D.C.L. in 1622.

[2] Also in B.M. Harl. 7340, f. 39 (written 1715–20 by Tudway: composer again given

[3] Litany only.

[4] Suffrages (i.e. from the close of the Paternoster, which is set in all these cases so that the choir picks up in the old traditional style at 'sed libera nos a malo', to the end. This was the practice before 1661.)

[5] The music ceases just before the end of the Benedicite.

FORMER SET							COMPOSER, TITLE AND REFERENCES	LATTER SET						
DECANI				CANTORIS				DECANI				CANTORIS		
Med.	MS. 39 CTI	CTII	MS. 38 B	MS. 34 Med.	CTI	MS. 33 B		MS. 44 Med.	MS. 42 CT	MS. 35 T	MS. 37 B	MS. 45 Med.	MS. 43 T	MS. 36 B
124							Behold it is Christ	T4	Q5	X2	Q4	118	S2	S1
	127	81	124	117	112	120	Behold now praise the Lord (8 voices)							
123							Fret not thyself	U6	R5	Y3	Q12	124ᵛ	T3	T4
121	126		127	120			O God my heart is ready (5 voices)							
121ᵛ	130	73	123	118	114	118	Praise the Lord O my soul [Lich.]							
	130ᵛ		123ᵛ	118ᵛ	114ᵛ	119	Tell the daughter of Sion							
125ᵛ	133ᵛ		131ᵛ	125ᵛ	118	126	Thou art worthy O Lord							
	129ᵛ		125	117ᵛ	113		To Jesus Christ the faithful witness	D6	L1	G6				
							Truly God is loving unto Israel	E6(2)	I7	L4(2)	M5(2)	19		W2
120	128		129	119	111	117	Turn thee again O Lord							
117ᵛ 122	125	74	128	121			Unto thee lift I up mine eyes							

27

| LATTER SET | | | | | | | COMPOSER, TITLE AND | FORMER SET | | | | | | |
| CANTORIS | | | DECANI | | | | REFERENCES | DECANI | | | | CANTORIS | | |
MS. 36 B	MS. 43 T	MS. 45 Med.	MS. 37 B	MS. 35 T	MS. 42 CT	MS. 44 Med.		— Med.	MS. 39 CT I	— CT II	MS. 38 B	MS. 34 Med.	— CT I	MS. 33 B
							LUGG, John. *Vicar-choral of Exeter in 1634.*							
N5	F2	53v	K3	N5v	F5	F2	Behold how good and joyful							
N5v	F2v	53	K3v	N5	F5v	F1	Let my complaint							
							MACE, Thomas. 1613–1709							
							I heard a voice[1]		172v		173	160v		159
							MARSON, John							
							God is our hope and strength				161			
					O4	Q1	O clap your hands							
							MOLLE, Henry. *Organist of Peterhouse*							
G2v	M6[3]	73		C3	O3v	K3	First Service (? 1636): Mag., Nd. Tud.	19	19v 102(2)v		61	17v[2] 121v	18v	19v
	F1	22	F1	F4	F6	K3v Q3(3)v	Second Service: Mag., Nd. Tud.							101v

[1] This seems to be the only scrap of composition surviving from the hand of this famous musical writer. He was one of the clerks of Trinity College, and this may have been a very early work of his: it is the last item in the Former Set.　　[2] Two verses only.　　[3] Nunc dimittis only.

FORMER SET — DECANI				FORMER SET — CANTORIS			COMPOSER, TITLE AND REFERENCES	LATTER SET — DECANI				LATTER SET — CANTORIS		
— Med.	**MS. 39 CTI**	**— CTII**	**MS. 38 B**	**MS. 34 Med.**	**— CTI**	**MS. 33 B**		**MS. 44 Med.**	**MS. 42 CT**	**MS. 35 T**	**MS. 37 B**	**MS. 45 Med.**	**MS. 43 T**	**MS. 36 B**
							Latin Te Deum	D6v	C7 K5	R4	F5(2) H2v	57		G5
							Latin Litany	BI	A6	L5	A2	50(2)	A2	GI
							English Litany ('Dr Cozens')	B6v	A3	L6v B5	B5(Iv)	B3	M2v	A2
105	112		109	103	100	103	Great and marvellous							
							MORLEY, Thomas. 1557–?1603							
89	97		95	88		89	First Service: TD, Btus, Ky., Cr., Mag., Nd. _Barn._	U4	R4	Y2	Q10	122	T2	T3
137v	148						Second Service: Mag., Nd. _Barn._			C4[1]		5		
				134	128	124	How long wilt thou forget me							K6
							Out of the deep _Barn._	I1	F2	N3	K4	AI	GI	N6
							Teach me thy way O Lord	RI	PI	T10	O9	102	P5	Q4

[1] End of Magnificat, and Nunc dimittis.

FORMER SET							COMPOSER, TITLE AND REFERENCES	LATTER SET						
DECANI				CANTORIS				DECANI				CANTORIS		
— Med.	MS. 39 CTI	— CTII	MS. 38 B	MS. 34 Med.	— CTI	MS. 33 B		MS. 44 Med.	MS. 42 CT	MS. 35 T	MS. 37 B	MS. 45 Med.	MS. 43 T	MS. 36 B
							MUDD, Thomas. ? c. 1560–1620[1]							
							I will alway give thanks [Lich.]	E2v		G3v	H3v	33v	H3v	L3
							O clap your hands	E3v		G5	H5	35	H4v	L5
							MUNDY, John. d. 1630							
25	29	30v	30	27	25	30v	Psalms for Ascension Day, Morning (viii, xv and xxi)[2]							
							First Service: TD, Btus, Ky., Cr., Mag., Nd. Barn.	N2	K6	M4	E3	80	O4	E3
							Lay not up for yourselves (Offertory sentence)	N5						
		22	16			152	Service in 3 parts for men: TD, Btus, Mag., Nd.		D4	E3	C4		C1	C3
							TD, Btus							
							Mag., Nd.		E1	E6	C6		C6v	
							Service in 4 parts for men: TD, Btus, Ky., Cr., Mag., Nd.		C3	D5	C3		B1	B2 (No Ky. or Cr.)

[1] Named as Thomas, though Jebb for some reason thought it should be the John Mudd who died about 1639.

[2] With Preces by Edward Smith, q.v.

	FORMER SET						COMPOSER, TITLE AND REFERENCES	LATTER SET						
DECANI				CANTORIS				DECANI				CANTORIS		
Med.	MS. 39 CTI	CTII	MS. 38 B	MS. 34 Med.	CTI	MS. 33 B		MS. 44 Med.	MS. 42 CT	MS. 35 T	MS. 37 B	MS. 45 Med.	MS. 43 T	MS. 36 B
35v	72		67	62	52v	75v	Short Service: TD, Jub., Ky., Cr. [St Johns]							
							Ky. only	B2v	B1v	B6v	A3v			
38	52[1] 53		41	36[2]	37	40	Evening Service *in medio chori*, 9 parts: Mag., Nd.							
42	55v	37	46	40v	39v	43	Evening Service *in medio chori*:[3] Mag., Nd.							
							Evening Service in C fa ut	T1	Q3	W6(2)	Q1	115	R6	
							Blessed is God in all his gifts		O2	Q1v	O3	74	N6	P2(2v)
							Give laud unto the Lord	T5	Q6	X3	Q5	119	S3v	S2 (medius part)
							This is my commandment		G3	G1	I6		G6	N1
							PALMER, Henry							
30v	34v	33	32v	29	30v	26	Preces and Psalm for Easter Day at Evensong							
21	20v		165	19	19v	16	Kyrie and Creed							

[1] Separate first and second contratenor on ff. 52, 53.
[2] Separate first and second treble on one page.
[3] 'Magnificat and Nunc dimittis to Mr Parson's Service of five parts.'

Composer, Title and References	LATTER SET DECANI				LATTER SET CANTORIS			FORMER SET DECANI			FORMER SET CANTORIS	
	MS. 44 Med.	MS. 42 CT	MS. 35 T	MS. 37 B	MS. 45 Med.	MS. 43 T	MS. 36 B	MS. 39 CTI Med.	— CTII	MS. 38 B	MS. 34 Med. — CTI	MS. 33 B
PALMER, Henry (*continued*)												
Lord what is man / *Organ-Book* 3	G5	D3	K1	H1	42	K1	M2					
PARSLEY, Osbert. 1511–85												
Short Service: TD, Btus[1]	M1	M5	S5	D6	92^v	C3	I2^v					
PARSONS, Robert, *of Exeter. c.* 1535–70												
(First) Service: TD, Btus, Ky, Cr, Mag., Nd. [St. Johns], Batt.	S2	Q2	W2	P5	108	Q4	R4					
Flat Service						C3						
Ever blessed Lord ('Collect for the Quire')[2]	S63	Q2 (5)[3]	W63	P94	112^v	R3^v	R4(4)					
O bone Jesu	P1		O4	N2	67	N2						
PATRICK, Nathaniel												
Service: TD, Btus, Mag., Nd.	L3	M1^v	S1	D3	88	N4	H4					

[1] Printed in *Tudor Church Music*, x, 271.
[2] Dated in Tenor Cantoris, 25 June 1639; and probably by a later composer of the same name.
[3] No words or music written.
[4] First line of words and music only.

FORMER SET							COMPOSER, TITLE AND REFERENCES	LATTER SET						
DECANI				CANTORIS				DECANI				CANTORIS		
Med.	MS. 39 CTI	CTII	MS. 38 B	MS. 34 Med.	CTI	MS. 33 B		MS. 44 Med.	MS. 42 CT	MS. 35 T	MS. 37 B	MS. 45 Med.	MS. 43 T	MS. 36 B
							PHILIPS, Peter. *d. c.* 1633							
							Aspice Domine quia facta[1]	P4			M4(3)v	68		
							PIERSON, Martin. *c.* 1580–1650							
97v	107v		103v	96v	94v	97v	Blow up the trumpet							
96	106		102	95	92	96	Bow down thine ear							
							PORTMAN, Richard. *d.* 1659. *Organist of Westminster Abbey*, 1633–42							
							Full Service in G: Ven., TD, Btus, Ky., Cr., Mag., Nd. [Lamb, St Johns], Tud.	Q5v[2]	O6(2)	T6	O5	99v	P4	Q3
						32v	Lord who shall dwell Batt.	U3	R3	Y1	Q9	121v	T1	T2
							O God my heart is ready	W2	R6v	Y4v	R2	126	T4v	T5v
							RAMSEY, Robert. *Mus.Bac.* 1616. *Organist of Trinity College*, 1628–44							
148v	159v 158(2)		152v				Service in 4 parts: TD, Jub., Ky., Cr., Mag., Nd. Tud.							

[1] Authorship given at f. 2v of Bass Decani.   ² No Venite.

LATTER SET							COMPOSER, TITLE AND REFERENCES	FORMER SET						
CANTORIS			DECANI					CANTORIS			DECANI			
MS. 36 B	MS. 43 T	MS. 45 Med.	MS. 37 B	MS. 35 T	MS. 42 CT	MS. 44 Med.		MS. 33 B	— CTI	MS. 34 Med.	MS. 38 B	— CTII	MS. 39 CTI	— Med.
							RAMSEY, Robert (*continued*)							
							Litany in D mi. from the same Service Jebb II	152	142	152v	154		159(2)v	149
			B3	B2	A4v	A4v	Another Litany							
G6v	N2	58	F6	G6v	G3(2)	A3	Latin Te Deum and Jubilate in F ma. (No. 1)							
H1(2)	N3(5)	64	F8	H1(4v)	K5(5)	K8	Latin Te Deum and Jubilate in F ma. (No. 2)							
P6	O3	79	N5(2)	Q4(2)	O4(3)	Q3(3)	Latin Litany Jebb II							
			I2(2)v			E1v	Collect for Christmas Day						135v	
							Collect for Easter Day			75v 145v	113v			
							Collect for Ascension Day	141v	138	146	149v		100 117 158	146v
	K6		I2(2)				Collect for Whitsunday	142	138v	146v	149v		158v	147
							Collect for Trinity Sunday	142v	139	147	150		159	147v

FORMER SET							COMPOSER, TITLE AND REFERENCES	LATTER SET						
DECANI				CANTORIS				DECANI				CANTORIS		
— Med.	MS. 39 CTI	— CTII	MS. 38 B	MS. 34 Med.	— CTI	MS. 33 B		MS. 44 Med.	MS. 42 CT	MS. 35 T	MS. 37 B	MS. 45 Med.	MS. 43 T	MS. 36 B
138^v	149^v			128^v			Collect for the Purification of B.V.M.				G7^v		K4(2)	L1
			132^v				Collect for the Annunciation of B.V.M.			A5^v				
	136		151	132 139^v	121	143	Collect for All Saints' Day							L5^v
128^v	161		156^v	124^v			I heard a voice from heaven							
151^v			126^v			148	My song shall be alway							
							O sapientia	C5 13^v	I1^v	K3^v		5^v 45^v	L2^v	N3^v
							SHEPHERD, John. *Organist of Magdalen College, Oxford, 1542–51. d. ? 1562*							
							I give you a new commandment[1]		G2	F6	F4		F4	
							SMITH, Edward. *Organist of Durham, 1609–11. d. 1611*							
25	29	30^v	30	27	25	30^v	Preces, with Mundy's Psalms for Ascension Day[2]							
26	29^v	31	31^v	27^v	26	30	Same Preces, with Psalms for All Saints' Day							

[1] In Day's *Certaine Notes* (1560 and 1565), and in *The Parish Choir* (1848), II, 115. One of the psalms of Gibbons (q.v.) is also ascribed to Edward Smith at Bass Decani, f. 38.

[2] The ascription of the Psalms to Mundy follows Jebb: as they are clearly marked Edward Smith in the MSS., Jebb presumably had good reasons for the ascription.

FORMER SET							COMPOSER, TITLE AND REFERENCES	LATTER SET						
DECANI				CANTORIS				DECANI				CANTORIS		
— Med.	MS. 39 CTI	— CTII	MS. 38 B	MS. 34 Med.	— CTI	MS. 33 B		MS. 44 Med.	MS. 42 CT	MS. 35 T	MS. 37 B	MS. 45 Med.	MS. 43 T	MS. 36 B
							SMITH, Edward (*continued*)							
135	146		162	136ᵛ	126	123	O praise God in his holiness Batt.	H1ᵛ			H1ᵛ		K2	
							SMITH, John							
94(2)	102(3)		101	93(2)		94	Morning Service: TD, Brus							
							SMITH, William. *Organist of Durham,* 1588–98							
27	30ᵛ	28	25	21	27	27	Preces¹ and Psalm for Christmas Day, Matins Jebb I (Preces only)							
27ᵛ	31ᵛ	29	26	22	28	27	Psalm for Christmas Day, Evensong							
28ᵛ	33	27	26ᵛ	25	29	28ᵛ	Psalm for Easter Day, Matins							
29	32ᵛ	29ᵛ	27ᵛ	32(2)ᵛ	29ᵛ	29	Psalm for Whitsunday, Matins							
							Preces and Responses	C4	B3ᵛ	C5ᵛ	A5ᵛ	A4ᵛ	A1ᵛ	G3ᵛ
81ᵛ	89	50ᵛ	87ᵛ	81ᵛ	79	83	I will wash my hands *Organ-Book* 21							

¹ The same Preces are written in some of the part-books for the other Proper Psalms.

36

COMPOSER, TITLE AND REFERENCES	LATTER SET — DECANI MS. 44 Med.	DECANI MS. 42 CT	DECANI MS. 35 T	DECANI MS. 37 B	CANTORIS MS. 45 Med.	CANTORIS MS. 43 T	CANTORIS MS. 36 B	FORMER SET — DECANI Med.	DECANI MS. 39 CTI	DECANI CTII	DECANI MS. 38 B	CANTORIS MS. 34 Med.	CANTORIS —CTI	CANTORIS MS. 33 B
If the Lord himself								98	108		104ᵛ	97	95	98ᵛ
STEVENSON, Robert. *b. c. 1542 Organist of Chester, 1569–1602. Mus.Doc. Oxon. 1596*														
When the Lord turned again								34ᵛ	40ᵛ	35	36	35	34ᵛ	33
STONARD, William. *Mus.Bac. Oxon. 1608 and Organist of Christ Church. d. 1630*														
Hear O my people *Organ-Book 7*	L1		M3	H6(2)	56	G5	M1							
Sing unto God *Organ-Book 9*	L1ᵛ		M3ᵛ	H6(3)	56ᵛ	G5ᵛ	M1							
When the sorrows of hell *Organ-Book 8*	L1			H6(2ᵛ)			M1ᵛ							
STROGERS, Nicholas														
Short Service: Ven., TD, Btus, Ky., Cr., Mag., Nd. [Ely (Organ-Book)], Barn.								43ᵛ	46		47	41ᵛ	42	36
Domine non est exaltatum	O1		R2	M1	72	D2[1] D6[2]	C6							
O God be merciful unto us and bless us								32ᵛ	36ᵛ	34ᵛ	35ᵛ	34	33	33ᵛ

[1] Ky., Cr., Mag., Nd.   [2] Ven., TD, Btus.

FORMER SET						COMPOSER, TITLE AND REFERENCES	LATTER SET						
DECANI		CANTORIS					DECANI				CANTORIS		
MS. 39 CTI (Med.)	CTII	MS. 38 B	MS. 34 Med.	CTI	MS. 33 B		MS. 44 Med.	MS. 42 CT	MS. 35 T	MS. 37 B	MS. 45 Med.	MS. 43 T	MS. 36 B
						TALLIS, Thomas. c. 1505–85 [1]							
5		5	5		4	Preces and Responses — Jebb I							
						Second Preces and Responses	B3(2)	A1	C2				A2
						'Dorian' Service: TD, Btus, Ky., Cr., Mag., Nd. — Boyce	L5	M3	S3	D5	90	E2	H6
						The same, with Venite added — Barn.					I4		D4
						Litany	A5	B6v	B3	B4			
						Kyrie only	B2	B1	B6	A3			
						Sanctus and Gloria	D1v	F1	O1	C1	A2(2)	G2	A5
						Lamentations I	P3v		P1v	N3v			
						Lamentations II	P2		P2	N3(2)			
						Adesto nunc propitius	P5		P3v	N4	68v		
						Arise O Lord	G4	D2v	A2v				

[1] The Latin works of Tallis are to be found in *Tudor Church Music*, VI (1928).

DECANI			CANTORIS					DECANI				CANTORIS		
Med. (—)	MS. 39 CTI	CTII (—)	MS. 38 B	MS. 34 Med.	CTI (—)	MS. 33 B	COMPOSER, TITLE AND REFERENCES	MS. 44 Med.	MS. 42 CT	MS. 35 T	MS. 37 B	MS. 45 Med.	MS. 43 T	MS. 36 B
							Discomfit them, O Lord[1]	D2 / R1v	E6 / P1v	L4 / T10v	O9v	102v	P5v	O3 / Q4v
			126		115	121	Hear the voice and prayer							
							O God be merciful[1]	F3	F4	I1v	G4			
	157(2)		152	148			Verily verily I say unto you							
							TAVERNER, John. d. 1545							
							Missa (Sine nomine)[2]	O3		O2 / O5	M4		G3	
							TOMKINS, Thomas. d. 1656							
				122v			Preces and Responses[3] Jebb II	B3(2)v	A1v	C2v	B3v			A2v
	62v[5]		71v	64v	70	51	First Service:[4] TD, Btus, Ky., Cr., Mag., Nd.	M2v[6]						
	69	42	70	62(2)	61	60	Venite				A3v			
	63						Kyrie only	B2v	B1v	B6v				
	69						(First) Litany Jebb II	A6v	A5	B2		A3v		A3v

[1] Adapted from his 'Absterge Domine' (*Tudor Church Music*, VI, 180).
[2] In an early 16th-century hand. See also in the Henrician part-books above (p. 2), folios 25, 23v, 29, 24.
[3] Jebb in his MS. Catalogue of 1853 says 'The Preces resemble those in his *Musica Deo Sacra* but the Responses are not there'. Preces only are in *Tudor Church Music*, VIII, 3.
[4] *Tudor Church Music*, VIII, 17.
[5] Magnificat and Nunc dimitis only.
[6] First part of Te Deum only.

FORMER SET DECANI · Med. (—)	MS. 39 CTI	CTII (—)	MS. 38 B	CANTORIS · MS. 34 Med.	CTI (—)	MS. 33 B	COMPOSER, TITLE AND REFERENCES	LATTER SET DECANI · MS. 44 Med.	MS. 42 CT	MS. 35 T	MS. 37 B	CANTORIS · MS. 45 Med.	MS. 43 T	MS. 36 B
							TOMKINS, Thomas (continued)							
							(Second) Litany — Jebb II	A6	A4	B4	B3	A3	A3	
							Collect for Whitsunday[1]	I2(3)	F3	N6	I1	2	F4	M3
	132		127	132		127	Collect for All Saints' Day[1]				L4			
							Behold the hour cometh[1]		K3	L3	L5			
32	36	33ᵛ	35ᵛ	30	32	32	Blessed be the Lord God[1]							F6
33	37ᵛ		34ᵛ	34ᵛ	33ᵛ	34ᵛ	Give sentence with me[1]							
			139				Jesus came when the doors were shut — Organ-Book 14	F4	L2	A5		37	I2	M4
							My beloved spake[1]	W1	R6	Y4	R1	125	T4	T5
128	140	78	134	128	123	130	O Lord I have loved[1]							
143	154		146ᵛ	142ᵛ	134	139	O pray for the peace of Jerusalem[1]							

[1] Printed in Tomkins' *Musica Deo Sacra* (1668).

| LATTER SET | | | | | | | | FORMER SET | | | | | | |
| CANTORIS | | | DECANI | | | | | CANTORIS | | | DECANI | | | |
MS. 36 B	MS. 43 T	MS. 45 Med.	MS. 37 B	MS. 35 T	MS. 42 CT	MS. 44 Med.	COMPOSER, TITLE AND REFERENCES	MS. 33 B	— CTI	MS. 34 Med.	MS. 38 B	— CTII	MS. 39 CTI	— Med.
R6	S1	117	Q3	X1	Q4	T3	Sing unto God[1]							
K5v	K3v						Thou art my King, O God[1]	124	127v	133v			148	137
T1v	S6v		Q8v	X6v	R2v	U2v	Turn unto the Lord our God							
							TYE, Christopher. d. 1572/3							
L1v	L1		G3		I5	G6	Evening Service. Mag., Nd.[2]			132v				
O7			M3	R3v			Miserere mei Deus[3]							
							Praise the Lord ye children[4]	149		149	158			
							WARD, John. 1580–before 1641							
S6	S5		Q7	X5	R1	U1	I heard the voice of a great multitude							
							Let God arise Barn.	131v	99	102	108		111[5]	103

[1] Printed in Tomkin's *Musica Deo Sacra* (1668).
[2] Printed in Rimbault's *Services*.
[3] Also in Christ Church, Oxford, MSS. 979–83 and British Museum MSS. Addit. 5059, f. 38.
[4] *Tudor Church Music*, octavo series, no. 58, ed. A. Ramsbotham.
[5] After the name of 'Mr Ward' has been added 'Mr ffrisney': and below is a further comment in the same hand, well-formed and too mature to be merely that of a choir-boy, 'Mr ffrisney wore his heire at length'.

FORMER DECANI — Med.	FORMER DECANI MS. 39 CTI	FORMER DECANI CTII	FORMER DECANI MS. 38 B	FORMER CANTORIS MS. 34 Med.	FORMER CANTORIS CTI	FORMER CANTORIS MS. 33 B	COMPOSER, TITLE AND REFERENCES	LATTER DECANI MS. 44 Med.	LATTER DECANI MS. 42 CT	LATTER DECANI MS. 35 T	LATTER DECANI MS. 37 B	LATTER CANTORIS MS. 45 Med.	LATTER CANTORIS MS. 43 T	LATTER CANTORIS MS. 36 B
							WARWICK, Thomas. *Organist of Hereford, 1586–9; of the Chapel Royal from 1625*							
							O God of my salvation	T5v	Q6v	X3v	Q5v	119v	S3	S2v (*medius pars*)
							WEELKES, Thomas. *d.* 1623							
51v	41v 57v		53v	51	49	45v	Service of 4 parts: Mag., Nd.					114	R5	R5
52v	60[1] 43		54	53	51	46	Service of 5 parts for 2 trebles: Mag., Nd. Batt.							
130	142	80	137				Service of 7 parts: Mag., Nd.							
							O how amiable							
							WHITE, Robert. *c.* 1530–74[2]							
							O how glorious art thou	Q2v	H5v	Q2v	O1v	74	N6	P3v
107v	114v		111v	105v		107v	O praise God in his holiness *Organ-Book* 23							

[1] First and second Contratenor on ff. 60 and 43.

[2] For details about the claims of Matthew, Robert and William White to these three anthems see *Tudor Church Music*, v (1926), Introduction, pp. xxiv–xxxviii. Jebb gave all three to Matthew, but the ascriptions above seem to be reasonably certain, except for 'O praise God', which has some MS. evidence in favour of William. This is printed at *Tudor Church Music*, v, 207, 211; 'O how glorious' at p. 197.

FORMER SET							COMPOSER, TITLE AND REFERENCES	LATTER SET						
DECANI				*CANTORIS*				*DECANI*				*CANTORIS*		
— Med.	MS. 39 CTI	CTII	MS. 38 B	MS. 34 Med.	— CTI	MS. 33 B		MS. 44 Med.	MS. 42 CT	MS. 35 T	MS. 37 B	MS. 45 Med.	MS. 43 T	MS. 36 B
							WHITE, William, *of Durham*[1]							
	143		138	131		110	Behold now, praise the Lord[2] *Organ-Book 35*					9		
							WILKINSON, Thomas							
							Kyrie[3] *(Tenor and Bass)*	H5	E4		O4			O5
33	35v		33v	31	31v	34	Behold O Lord[2]			I2				
126	135		132	130		119v	Hear my prayer, O Lord[4] [Lich.], Batt. Ely.			I4		42(2)	K5	
32	36v	33	34	30[6]	32v	32	Help Lord[5]							
							Lord I am not high-minded	D5						
152	161v		157			147	O Lord God of my salvation[7]							
							WILSON, Thomas. *Organist of Peterhouse*[8]							
							Psalm for Christmas Day, Morning (lxxxv) *Organ-Book 27*	B5	B5	D1	B1	52	M3v	

[1] See note 2 on p. 42 above.
[2] Also in British Museum, MSS. Addit. 30478-9.
[3] Following Child's Burial Service in each case. But there is no Creed, a detail which may or may not be liturgically suggestive.
[4] Also in British Museum, MSS. Addit. 29372-7 and Oxford, Christ Church, MSS. 56-60.
[5] Also in British Museum, MSS. Addit. 29366-8 and 30478-9.
[6] Music unfinished.
[7] Also in British Museum, MSS. Harley 7340-44b.
[8] Described on f. G2 of Bassus Cantoris by one of his admirers as 'Vir bonus haud pius'.

| | FORMER SET | | | | | COMPOSER, TITLE AND REFERENCES | LATTER SET | | | | | | |
| | DECANI | | CANTORIS | | | | DECANI | | | | CANTORIS | | |
	MS. 39 —Med. / CTI	CTII	MS. 38 B	MS. 34 Med. / CTI	MS. 33 B		MS. 44 Med.	MS. 42 CT	MS. 35 T	MS. 37 B	MS. 45 Med.	MS. 43 T	MS. 36 B
						WILSON, Thomas (*continued*)							
						Evening Service in C ma.: Mag., Nd.		S1		R2^v	126^v		T6
						Evening Service in A mi.: Mag., Nd.	Q3	O5	Y5^v	O2	76^v	T5	P4
						Venite	A5(2)			B6	A5(1)	A5	
						Venite (another, dated 1636)	Q5	O2(2)^v	M1^v				P2
						Latin Kyrie and Credo	O6	O2(2)	Q2	N6	75	N4(2)	
	155^v		150^v	147^v	144^v	Sanctus							P4^v
						Latin Litany							G1
						Collect for St John's Day		S2^v	Z1	R4	128	D1	T7^v
						Collect for the Circumcision			Z1^v	R4^v	128^v	U1	T8
						Behold how good and joyful			Z2	R4(2)	129	V1^v	T8^v

| | FORMER SET | | | | | | | LATTER SET | | | | | | |
| COMPOSER, TITLE AND REFERENCES | DECANI | | | | CANTORIS | | | DECANI | | | | CANTORIS | | |
	— Med.	MS. 39 CTI	— CTII	MS. 38 B	MS. 34 Med.	— CTI	MS. 33 B	MS. 44 Med.	MS. 42 CT	MS. 35 T	MS. 37 B	MS. 45 Med.	MS. 43 T	MS. 36 B
Behold now praise the Lord									S2	Y6ᵛ	R3ᵛ	127ᵛ	T6	T7
Blessed is the man									P3ᵛ		O4	77ᵛ	O1ᵛ	P5ᵛ
Christ rising again *Organ-Book 28*								H3	I6ᵛ		L6(2)	43	M6ᵛ	O6
Prevent us O Lord								Q3ᵛ	O5ᵛ	Q3ᵛ	O3ᵛ	77ᵛ		P5
Thy mercy O Lord	153			159		140	145							
Turn thy face from my sins	152ᵛ			159ᵛ		139ᵛ	150							
WOODSON, Leonard. d. 1641. *Organist of Eton,* 1615														
Give the king thy judgements	129	141		135¹ 136	129	125	131			B3ᵛ				
ANONYMOUS														
Venite: four parts in score					92									
[Venite]: five Gregorian chants (8ᶜ, 1ᵃ, 3ᵇ, 7ᶜ, 2ᵈ) for treble and tenor														

¹ f. 135, Chorus only; f. 136, called the 'Singing Part', has music for the Verse also.

	FORMER SET — DECANI				FORMER SET — CANTORIS			COMPOSER, TITLE AND REFERENCES	LATTER SET — DECANI				LATTER SET — CANTORIS		
	— Med.	MS. 39 CTI	— CTII	MS. 38 B	MS. 34 Med.	— CTI	MS. 33 B		MS. 44 Med.	MS. 42 CT	MS. 35 T	MS. 37 B	MS. 45 Med.	MS. 43 T	MS. 36 B
ANONYMOUS (continued)															
Glory be to the Father, &c. (5 parts in score)		124^{v1}													
Benedicite (Latin: condensed)		21^{v}		165^{v}	20				C6	E2	F3	G1	26		
Laudate Dominum omnes gentes[2]		21^{3}								O1	F1	M5	18^{4} 25		
Evening Service: Mag., Nd.											Q3			$N6^{v}$	
Ad te levavi											$(ii)^{v5}$	$(ii)^{v}$		$(i)^{v}$	$(i)^{v5}$
Aspice Domine de sanctis											(ii)	(ii)		(i)	(i)
Audite verbum Domini												(vi)			
Benedictus es Domine									$P4^{v}$		$(iii)^{v5}$	$(iii)^{v}$			$(ii)^{v5}$
Cantemus virgini												N4	68^{v}		
Coeli enarrant												$(iv)^{v}$			

[1] Unfinished.

[2] Evidently connected with the foregoing, as in the Elizabethan *Commemoratio Benefactorum*. The composer's name was written at f. 18 of Medius Cantoris, but only the first four letters of 'Rich[ard]' survive. There are five Richards in the Caroline part-books: Dering, Farrant, Hinde, Hutchinson and Portman. To no one of these can attribution be directed, except possibly the first: both music and handwriting are Caroline rather than Elizabethan.

[3] Opening only, "à 6 parts".

[4] f. 18 is the alto part, f. 25 the treble.

[5] Words only

FORMER SET							COMPOSER, TITLE AND REFERENCES	LATTER SET						
DECANI				CANTORIS				DECANI				CANTORIS		
—Med.	MS. 39 CTI	—CTII	MS. 38 B	MS. 34 Med.	—CTI	MS. 33 B		MS. 44 Med.	MS. 42 CT	MS. 35 T	MS. 37 B	MS. 45 Med.	MS. 43 T	MS. 36 B
							Estote fortes in bello				(iv)			(iii)
							Gaudeamus omnes				(v)			
	80^v		80^v	73^v		73	Hear my prayer ('For a basse')							
							In manus tuas Domine	O2		R1	M2	71		
							Let thy merciful ears						R5^v	R5^v
						158	Laudate Dominum in Sanctis				(v)^v			
							Lincoln Tune	W3^v			R5^v			
	172		172	160			O Jerusalem, Jerusalem			(iii)	(iii)			(ii)
							Omnes gentes plaudite							
							This is the day which the Lord hath made	W2^v	S3	Z2^v	R4(2)^v		U2	W2^v
							[Urbs coelestis Jerusalem]—no text	O6^v		P6	N1^v	70^v		
				115^v			(Wordless) Five parts in score							

3. THE ORGAN-BOOK (MS. 46)

The organ-book is not foliated, and the only means of identification is by the numbers of the items in order, as given below. They all correspond to entries in the vocal part-books of the Caroline sets, with the exception of nos. 10, 30, 31, and probably 13 and 36. The fact that the first three of these are all by Wilson, who was organist of Peterhouse, together with nos. 27 and 28, strongly suggests that he was the writer of the organ-book, or at least part of it.

Names and titles which appear in brackets are not given in the manuscript; they have been ascertained by comparison with the vocal part-books.

1.	Glory be to God on high	Amner
2.	This is the record of John	Gibbons
3.	Lord what is man (Psalms cxliv and cxlvi. 3, 4)	Palmer
4.	O Lord let me know mine end	(Batten)
5.	Have mercy upon me O God	Batten
6.	O sing unto the Lord	Hinde
7.	Hear O my people	Stonard
8.	When the sorrows of hell	Stonard
9.	Sing unto God	Stonard
10.	(bass only) ?	Wilson
11.	Ponder my word O Lord	Batten
12.	Praise the Lord O my soul	Batten
13.	?	?
14.	Jesus came (for St Thomas' Day)	Tomkins
15.	Hear my cry O God	Hilton
16.	O God of gods	Hooper
17.	Collect for Christmas Day	(Hooper)
18.	Thou art worthy O Lord	(Loosemore)
19.	Great Service, Magnificat and Nunc dimittis	Byrd
20.	We praise thee O Father	Gibbons
21.	I will wash my hands	Wm. Smith
22.	Behold it is Christ	(Hooper)
23.	O praise God in his holiness	(White)
24.	O Lord make thy servant Charles	Byrd
25.	Sing joyfully	Byrd
26.	O God the proud are risen	(Byrd)
27.	Lord thou art become gracious	Wilson
28.	(Christ rising again)	(Wilson)

29.	O God be merciful unto us	Strogers
30.	Collect for the 2nd Sunday in Lent, 5 parts	Wilson
31.	Collect for the 4th Sunday in Lent, 5 parts	Wilson
32.	Call to remembrance	(Hilton)
33.	O God (Lord) give ear	(Byrd)
34.	Rejoice in the Lord	Jeffries
35.	Behold now praise the Lord	White
36.	?	?

4. THE FOLIO PRAYER BOOK

Printed Book G. 5. 30 in the Perne Library is a fine folio copy of the Book of Common Prayer printed by Barker in 1634. Portions of the volume have been interleaved with pages of music-staves ruled by hand, and many of these pages have been filled in with the Medius Decani part of various settings from the Caroline part-books. Others are left with blank staves.

The book betrays evidence of a comprehensive plan, abandoned before it was finished: for though the table below, taken by itself, looks complete, the impression left by the actual volume with its half-empty pages of music is unmistakable. It may have been the troubles of the Great Rebellion which caused the noting of this splendid book to cease: or it may have been found that the design was over-ambitious and impracticable. The selection of music is most interesting, for it is evidently planned as a sort of basic *Ordinarium* to which the choir would add more florid music at festival times. The contents are as follows:

Preces and Responses: Byrd (third set): Tomkins (first set) and William Smith.

Preces only: The second Preces of Gibbons, with an alternative Gloria Patri.

Venite, Te Deum and Benedictus: Gibbons, Short Service.

The Litany: (i) Tallis; (ii) Tomkins—called 'Common Litany'; (iii) 'Mr Molle for Dr Cosin'.

Kyries 'Ad X Praecepta': (i) Byrd; (ii) Gibbons; (iii) Tallis; (iv) Farrant—the Short Service in each case; (v) Derrick; (vi) Tomkins; (vii) Amner—from 'Caesar's Service'; (viii) Child; (ix) Morley—First Service; (x) 'Monday'—Mundy's First Service.

Creed: Gibbons, Short Service.

Sanctus: Hooper, preceded by responses to Sursum corda, perhaps also by Hooper.

Gloria in excelsis: Amner.

Magnificat and Nunc dimittis: Gibbons, Short Service.

The Litany, in Latin: (i) 'Mr Molle pro Coll. Sti. Petri'; (ii) Loosemore—from his First Service in D minor. Both these litanies set only the old response at the end of a solo Lord's Prayer—'sed libera nos a malo': whereas the contemporary Oxford Convocation litany sets the whole prayer as a chorus in monotone with a four-part Amen.[1]

Bound up with this Prayer Book are the offices of Morning and Evening Prayer in Latin, in a fine folio printing paged 1 to 24 and apparently following the official (Haddon) edition of 1560: though Jebb in his manuscript catalogue says, 'The translation of the Mattins and Evensong differs, it is believed, from any now extant'. He also remarks, 'As far as the compiler of this volume is aware, nothing of this particular version [of the Litanies] has been discovered, beyond what is preserved in these musical adaptations of the suffrages'.

The typographical history of Latin editions of the Prayer Book does not seem to have been fully investigated, so that it would be rash to claim this folio Latin version as an unique specimen. But it does not seem to be mentioned elsewhere. There is some basic information in Blunt's *Annotated Book of Common Prayer* (1892), p. 104. W. Muss-Arnott, of Boston, U.S.A., gives some more specialized details in *The Prayer-book among the Nations* (London, S.P.C.K., 1914), but his treatment is not intended to be exhaustive, being confined to bibliographical accounts of a private collection in America. The latest printers before 1634 (the date of the main English part of this volume) seem to be John Norton—Muss-Arnott only mentions an octavo edition from him, dated 1604—and Henry Hall, who printed a duodecimo for Christ Church, Oxford, in 1615. Our Latin section here was executed, as the State Prayers demonstrate, during the reign of Charles I, but the authorities at the University Library are unable to trace the printer.

In this Latin section four pages of music-paper between 'Ad Matutinas' and 'Ad Vesperas' are left blank, but they are followed at once by the two Latin litanies of Molle and Loosemore. Evidently the use of Latin for Morning Prayer and Litany, with the Kyrie and Creed of the Communion Service, was either contemplated or (more likely) carried out, in accordance with the provisions of

[1] According to Jebb, *Choral Responses*.

the Act of Uniformity. There is only one example of the Kyrie and Creed in Latin, that by Thomas Wilson, who was organist of Peterhouse. The 'Kyrie' (Responses to the Commandments) follows the Elizabethan translation, but the Creed is taken without verbal change from the Missal, including the phrase 'unam *sanctam* catholicam et apostolicam ecclesiam'. One Latin mass appears entire—Taverner's *Sine nomine*: but the index to MS. 37 on f. 2ᵛ indicates that this was used as a source upon which to draw for anthem-music.

It is also interesting to notice in this connexion that the Perne Library contains a small number of octavo Prayer Books of contemporary date (1639), uniform and evidently the remains of a Chapel set. They too contain a Latin section, but in this case it takes the form of a Psalter, evidently printed abroad, for it contains the Monastic Canticles as well as those of the Book of Common Prayer, with the original doxology to the Benedicite which runs 'Benedicamus Patrem et Filium cum Sancto Spiritu...' instead of the usual Gloria Patri of the English and Latin editions of the Prayer Book. Before the first leaf, which is signed A1, a 'false title' imprinted A2 (another A2 follows the authentic A1) gives the table of psalms for the days of the month according to the Prayer Book arrangement, thus covering the papist importation with a decent Anglican cloak. The printer of this Psalter conveniently provided the numbering of the psalms according to the Hebrew method (with which the English Prayer Book agrees) as well as the Latin, thus making the edition entirely convenient for use in Peterhouse chapel.

INDEX OF TEXTS

The canticles of Morning and Evening Prayer, with or without the Responses to the Commandments and the Nicene Creed, occur throughout the Caroline part-books so frequently that it is pointless to index them under 'texts'. They are therefore omitted here. Items of infrequent occurrence which may be of some interest are listed at the head of the index, together with a table of the Collects used as anthems and of the 'salmi concerti', or proper psalms set anthemwise or nearly so.

Scrupulosity over the *ipsissima verba* of the Book of Common Prayer would seem to be a nineteenth-century invention. Our composers took such slight liberties as they thought fit. For example, if the verse 'Lord, let me know mine end' is searched for in this index it will be discovered under 'O Lord let me know mine end' as set by Adrian Batten.

Latin and English are indexed together. In 1856 Jebb, though a 'High Churchman', preferred to separate them with some care and to allude to some of the Latin works as 'proper to the unreformed service'. There seems no need to keep up this division.

The original manuscripts have tables of contents, written before the collections were completed: they are thus described by Jebb:

1. 'Ad Domine labia': i.e. the Preces, or Versicles before the Psalms.
2. 'Psalmi Festivales': or, the Psalms arranged like Canticles, such as we find in many of the older services, used on great festivals: a feature of the Choral Service now obsolete.
3. The 'Venite Exultemus' arranged as a Canticle.
4. 'Ad Dominus vobiscum': or, the Responses after the Creed.
5. 'Litanies', English and Latin.
6. 'Full Services'; under the three heads of 'Ad Matutinas', 'Ad Officium Altaris' (consisting of Kyrie and Creed; including also, in a few instances, the 'Glory' before the Gospel, and an Offertory sentence), and of 'Ad Vespertinas'.
7. 'Verse Services'; with the same threefold division.
8. 'Full Anthems'; in three divisions; 'Of praise'; 'Of prayer'; 'Of penitence'.
9. 'Verse Anthems'; similarly classed.
10. 'Ad Sursum Corda': and 'Ad Gloria in excelsis'.
11. 'Antiphonae Festivales': being, for the most part, the proper Collects of the great Festivals.

ITEMS OF SERVICE-MUSIC

COLLECTS:

Christmas Day	Hooper	*page* 24
	Ramsey	34
St John's Day	Geeres	20
	Wilson	44
The Circumcision	Hooper	24
	Wilson	44
The Epiphany	Bull	14
Second Sunday in Lent	Wilson (organ only)	49
Fourth Sunday in Lent	Wilson (organ only)	49
Easter Day	Dering	18
	Ramsey	34
Ascension Day	Ramsey	34
Whitsunday	Giles	22
	Ramsey	34
	Tomkins	40
Trinity Sunday	Ramsey	34
Purification B.V.M.	Ramsey	35
Annunciation B.V.M.	Ramsey	35
All Saints	Child	17
	Ramsey	35
	Tomkins	40
Fourth collect at the end of the Communion service (Prevent us O Lord)	Byrd	16
	Wilson	45

PROPER PSALMS:

Christmas Day, morning	William Smith	36
	Wilson (lxxxv)	43
Christmas Day, evening	Amner	10
	William Smith	36
Easter Day, morning	William Smith	36
Easter Day, evening	Gibbons (lvii, 9–12 and cxviii, 19–24)	20
	Palmer	31
Ascension Day, morning	Mundy	30
Ascension Day, evening	Byrd (xxiv, 7–10)	14
	Este (xlvii)	19
	Marson (xlvii)	28
	Mudd (xlvii)	30
	Loosemore (cviii)	27
	Portman (cviii)	33

Whitsunday, morning	William Smith	*page* 36
Whitsunday, evening	Batten (civ)	13
	Gibbons (clxv, 1–14 and	20
	15–21 separately: perhaps	
	designed for morning and	
	evening use)	

The psalms above follow the order of those appointed in the Book of Common Prayer. There are also two sets which have no such authority; but proper psalms for other days were proposed by Cosin in the margin of his Durham prayer book.[1] These have, of course, no relation to Byrd's choice of Epiphany psalms, where Cosin proposed ii and lvii in the morning, lxxii and xcvii for evensong. His selection for All Saints' Day was i, xv, lxxxiv and xci in the morning, cxii, cxiii, cxix, 1–16, cxlv and cxlix in the evening. From this programme Edward Smith seems to have selected a modest eight verses.

Epiphany	Byrd (cxiv, 1–6, lv. 1–8, cxix, 33–40)
All Saints' Day	Edward Smith (cxix, 1–8)

For some notes on these psalm-settings see E. H. Fellowes, *William Byrd* (2nd ed. 1948), pp. 119–21.

ANTHEMS AND MOTETS

A stranger here	Amner	*page* 10
Absterge Domine (adapted from)	Tallis	39, n. 1
Ad te levavi	Anonymous	46
Adesto nunc propitius	Tallis	38
Aeterne laudis lilium	Fayrfax	3
Albanus (mass)	Fayrfax	2
Almighty God, who by the leading of a star[2]	Bull	14
Arise O Lord	Tallis	38
Aspice Domine de sanctis	Anonymous	46
Aspice Domine quia facta	Philips	33

[1] See J. H. Blunt, *The Book of Common Prayer Annotated* (1903), p. 114.

[2] The rest of the Collects from the Book of Common Prayer, which have been listed above, are not entered here as a rule, the chief reason being that they start indeterminately with the words 'O God', 'O Lord', 'Almighty God', etc., without close reliance on the text of the Prayer Book.

Attollite portas	Byrd	*page* 14, n. 4
Ave cujus conceptio	Ludford	3
Ave Dei Patris filia	Fayrfax	2
	Marbeck	3
	Taverner	2
Ave gratia plena Maria	Chamberlayne	3
Ave Maria	Mason	2
Ave Maria ancilla	Aston	3
	Ludford	3
Ave Maria mater Dei	Hunt	2
Ave Mariae divae matris	Aston	2
Ave rosa sine spina	Tallis	3
Ave vulnus lateris	Erley	3
Awake and stand up	Este	19
Behold how good and joyful	Hutchinson	25
	Lugg	28
	Wilson	45
Behold I bring you glad tidings	Byrd	15
	Gibbons	21
Behold it is Christ	Hooper	24
	Loosemore	27
Behold now praise the Lord	Loosemore	27
	White	43
	Wilson	45
Behold O Lord	Wilkinson	43
Behold the hour cometh	Tomkins	40
Behold thou hast made my days	Gibbons	21
Blessed are all those	Batten	11
Blessed be the Lord God	Tomkins	40
Blessed is God in all his gifts	Mundy	31
Blessed is the man	Wilson	45
Blow out (up) the trumpet	Este	19
	Pierson	33
Bow down thine ear	Child	17
	Pierson	33
Call to remembrance	Farrant	19
	Hilton	23
Cantemus virgini	Anonymous	46
Christ rising again	Batten	11
	Juxon	26
	Wilson	45
Christe Jesu (mass)	Rasar	2

Christi virgo (mass)	Ludford	*page* 3
Deliver us O Lord	Batten	12
Discomfit them O Lord	Tallis	39
Domine Jesu Christe	Ludford	3
Domine non est exaltatum	Strogers	37
Euge dicta	Norman	2
Ever blessed Lord	Parsons	32
Exsultet in hac die	Sturmys	2
Fac cum servo tuo	Byrd	15
Fac nobis Domine	Taverner	3
Fret not thyself	Loosemore	27
Gaude plurimum	Taverner	3
Gaude virgo mater Christi	Alen	2
	Aston	3
Give laud unto the Lord	Mundy	31
Give sentence with me	Tomkins	40
Give the king thy judgements	Child	17
	Woodson	45
Glorious and powerful God	Gibbons	22
God is our hope and strength	Marson	28
Great and marvellous	Molle	29
Have mercy upon me O God	Batten	12
	Giles	22
Have ye no regard	Ferrabosco	20
He that hath my commandments	Giles	22
Hear me O Lord	Fido	20
Hear my cry O God	Hilton	23
Hear my crying	Hutchinson	25
Hear my prayer O God	Batten	12
	Wilkinson	43
Hear my prayer O Lord	Anonymous	47
	Batten	12
Hear O Lord	Amner	10
Hear O my people	Child	17
	Stonard	37
Hear the voice and prayer	Tallis	39
Help Lord for the godly man ceaseth	Wilkinson	43
Holy, holy, holy	Batten	12
How doth the city	Amner	10
How long O Lord	Byrd	15
How long wilt thou forget me	Morley	29
I give you a new commandment	Shepherd	35

Teach me thy way	Morley	*page* 29
Tecum principium (mass)	Fayrfax	2
Tell the daughter of Sion	Loosemore	27
Terrenum sitiens	Edwards	2
The blessed Lamb	Hooper	24
Therefore with angels	Dering	18
This is my commandment	Mundy	31
This is the day which the Lord hath made	Anonymous	47
This is the record of John	Gibbons	22
Thou art my king O God	Tomkins	41
Thou art worthy O Lord	Loosemore	27
Thy mercy O Lord	Wilson	45
To Jesus Christ the faithful witness	Loosemore	27
Totius mundi domina	Martin	3
Trium regum	Catcott	2
Truly God is loving unto Israel	Loosemore	27
Turn thee again O Lord	Loosemore	27
Turn thou us	Batten	13
	Child	17
Turn thy face from my sins	Wilson	45
Turn unto the Lord our God	Tomkins	41
Unto thee lift I up mine eyes	Loosemore	27
Urbs coelestis Jerusalem	Anonymous	47
Vae nobis miseris	Mason	2
Veni Sancte Spiritus (mass)	Pygott	2
Verily verily I say unto you	Tallis	39
Vidi aquam	(? Ludford)	3
We praise thee O Father	Gibbons	22
What shall I render	Child	17
When the Lord turned again	Stevenson	37
When the sorrows of hell	Stonard	37
Who can tell how oft he offendeth	Beck	13
Woe is me	Amner	11
Ye that fear the Lord	Hutchinson	25

PETERHOUSE MUSIC

Two short representative specimens of the Peterhouse music are appended. Both are from the Caroline books, as no tenor parts have yet been found for the Henrician set except in the case of such writers as Fayrfax and Ludford, most of whose works are well documented elsewhere and are not specially associated with Peterhouse.

In the Caroline books the music of the great masters such as Byrd, Tallis, Tomkins and White has already been printed, so that choice is naturally directed towards the work of the local men, doubtless specially written for the Peterhouse choir. For an English anthem, Wilson's 'Christ rising again' (part I) will show the College organist's style: and as the Latin work is prominent in these books, Ramsey's 'O sapientia' is added. The list of works under Ramsey's name shows his preference for the more objective texts provided by the Calendar, from which he seems to have picked out the mention of 'O sapientia' on December 16th as worth attention; and he has given us this effective setting of the old Magnificat antiphon, in a style reminiscent of Dering rather than of Byrd or Palestrina.

CHRIST RISING AGAIN

THOMAS WILSON

* After the fourth bar Wilson's organ part contains nothing but the treble and bass lines.

9-2

* MS. is probably wrong here and has been amended for two bars.

O SAPIENTIA

ROBERT RAMSEY

Printed in the United States
By Bookmasters